Public Access Terminals
Determining Quantity Requirements

OCLC Library, Information, and Computer Science Series

[1]   *Online Public Access Catalogs: The User Interface*
        Charles R. Hildreth

2   *Public Library Administrators' Planning Guide to Automation*
        Donald J. Sager

3   *Public Access Terminals: Determining Quantity Requirements*
        John E. Tolle

Public Access Terminals
Determining Quantity Requirements

John E. Tolle

6565 Frantz Road
Dublin, Ohio 43017-0702

To Michelle, Mike, and Jody

Contents

List of Figures, ix

List of Tables, xi

Foreword, xiii

Preface, xv

Acknowledgments, xix

1. Introduction, 1

    1.1 Objectives, **1**
    1.2 Scope, **2**
    1.3 Background, **3**
    1.4 Basic Problem Structure, **4**

2. Data Collection, 9

    2.1 Locations and Time Periods, **9**
    2.2 Training of Collectors, **10**
    2.3 Data Collection Methodology, **11**
        2.3.1 Reference Desk and Circulation Desk, **11**
        2.3.2 Building Occupancy, **13**
        2.3.3 Card Catalog, **15**
        2.3.4 Terminals, **18**

3. Application of Probability Theory to Represent Observed Patterns of Terminal Use, 23

   3.1 Terminal Use Patterns: Observed Distributions, **23**
      3.1.1 Interarrival Patterns, **24**
      3.1.2 Service Patterns, **25**
   3.2 Theoretical Probability Distributions, **25**
      3.2.1 Pearson Type III Distribution, **26**
      3.2.2 Lognormal Distribution, **28**
      3.2.3 Parameter Estimation, **32**
   3.3 Testing of Theoretical Vs. Observed Distributions, **33**
   3.4 Regression Analysis to Predict Arrival and Service Demand, **34**
   3.5 Queuing Analysis, **38**
      3.5.1 Single Server, Exponential Interarrivals and Service Times, **40**
      3.5.2 Multiple Server, Exponential Interarrivals and Service Times, **45**
      3.5.3 Other Potential Models, **48**

4. Terminal Use Patterns and the Required Number of Terminals to Satisfy Demand: Results, 51

   4.1 Distribution of Interarrivals, **51**
   4.2 Distribution of Service Times, **52**
   4.3 Regression Analysis, **53**
   4.4 Queuing Models to Predict the Required Number of Terminals, **57**

5. Guidelines for Conducting a Terminal Requirements Study, 135

   5.1 Introduction and Scope, **135**
   5.2 Organizational Requirements, **137**
   5.3 Methodology and Analysis Procedures, **137**
      5.3.1 Data Collection, **137**
      5.3.2 Data Analysis, Model Selection, and Application, **141**
   5.4 Conclusions, **143**

Appendixes, 145

Selected References, 157

Index, 159

List of Figures

1-1   Demand/Capacity Curve Over Time for Patron Arrivals, **5**

1-2   Formation of Queue Over Time When Demand Exceeds
       Capacity, **5**

2-1   Data Collection Form for Reference and Circulation
       Activity, **12**

2-2   Data Collection Form for Building Occupancy
       (Gate Counts), **14**

2-3   Data Collection Form for Card Catalog Activity, **17**

2-4   Data Collection Form for Terminal Activity, **19**

3-1   Type III Distribution for Various Values of k, **28**

3-2   Normal and Lognormal Distributions, **30**

3-3   Lognormal Distribution for Different μ, **31**

3-4   Lognormal Distribution for Different σ^2, **31**

3-5   Scatter Diagram Showing Observed Terminal Use
       as a Function of Circulation Activity, **36**

3-6   Single Server Queuing System, **40**

3-7   Multiple Server Queuing System, **45**

4–1 to   Observed Vs. Theoretical Distributions: Interarrivals
4–40   (By Library), **60**

4–41 to   Mean Interarrival Times
4–44   (By Quarter), **80**

4–45 to   Mean Interarrival Times
4–49   (By Library), **82**

4–50 to   Observed Vs. Theoretical Distributions: Service Times
4–93   (By Library), **93**

4–94 to   Mean Service Times
4–98   (By Library), **115**

4–99 to   Mean Service Times
4–102   (By Quarter), **118**

4–103   Probability of Waiting in Queue Vs. Traffic Intensity ρ, **133**

5–1   Required Steps in Conducting a Terminal Requirements
          Study, **136**

List of Tables

3–1   Example of Queue Length Behavior as Traffic Intensity
        ρ Varies,   **43**

3–2   A Summary of Queuing Relationships for Exponential
        Interarrivals and Service Times and a Single Server,   **45**

3–3   Random Arrivals and Service for Multiple Service Stations
        (Lead Patron Moves to First Vacancy),   **46**

4–1 to Summary of Test Results for Observed Interarrivals
4–4   (By Quarter),   **85**

4–5   Summary of Interarrival Times and Chi-square Tests,   **89**

4–6 to Summary of Test Results for Service Times
4–9   (By Quarter),   **120**

4–10   Summary of Service Times and Chi-square Tests,   **124**

4–11   Summary of Regression Analysis,   **128**

4–12   Probability of Waiting in Queue $\leq$ Time t Is 0.90,   **130**

4–13   Probability of Waiting in Queue $\leq$ Time t Is 0.95,   **131**

4–14   Probability of Waiting in Queue $\leq$ Time t Is 0.99,   **132**

Foreword

In planning and implementing the transition to an
online public access catalog, there is no more
critical question to answer than how many terminals
are required to meet user needs satisfactorily. Even
with the best conceived, best designed,
user-friendliest online system, acceptance will be
seriously prejudiced if patrons must often wait in
long lines to gain access to the bibliographic
store--a condition which very seldom occurs in use of
card catalogs with as many "terminals" as there are
drawers. Concomitantly, given the high costs
involved, it is requisite not to install terminals in
such quantity that many will stand idle most of the
time.

It was with this problem in mind that The Ohio State
University Libraries, in the midst of planning such a
transition, approached research staff at OCLC, which
happily resulted in agreement to conduct a
collaborative study for which a National Science
Foundation grant was subsequently awarded.

This document conveys the results of that study; but,
more importantly, it provides guidelines on how to
replicate the research so that other libraries can
apply the same techniques to obtain answers pertinent
to their own settings within their own defined
parameters. Here, observed data (e.g., reference
activity, circulation volume, catalog access, patron

traffic) are used in conjunction with sound analytical techniques such as mathematical modeling and probability and queuing theories, to produce tangible, pragmatically applicable answers to how many terminals will do under what variable conditions. For OSU Libraries the results provided essential, key argumentation in convincing the administration to fund permanently the last 50 of our 114 public terminals, and, equally significant, gave us a reliable basis on where to place what number of terminals which had theretofore been distributed according to educated guesstimates.

In our view this research makes a major contribution in a crucial area where little, if any, relevant guidance is available; and OCLC is to be highly commended for its initiative and efforts. While perhaps not a perfect or definitive answer, libraries, with the assistance of this study, now have a usable, credible tool in attempting to predict terminal needs intelligently instead of by the seat of the pants.

William J. Studer
Director
The Ohio State University Libraries
August 1983

Preface

The basis for this monograph grew out of research that was conducted for a National Science Foundation project (#IST-7920312) entitled "Terminal Requirements for Online Catalogs in Libraries." Numerous persons expressed their personal and institutional desires to see the work published in a thorough manner and made available to those involved in determining the online terminal systems. Such effort was also suggested and encouraged by the National Science Foundation, who recognized the need to put together both the basic research required and the techniques available to analyze the required number of terminals when a library converts to or expands its online catalog.

This monograph is the third in the OCLC Library, Information, and Computer Science Series. It represents an expansion of the work done for the National Science Foundation and is organized into a form which will be of use to others in the library and information science field who wish to conduct studies of their systems. As such, it is presumed that it will encourage that a quantitative approach be taken to contribute to the decision-making process when considering online terminals. The study of other systems, in addition to providing the results to those involved in improving their own systems, will add to basic knowledge of how libraries are being used and will contribute to building sound empirical data toward a theory of library demand and service. This

in turn will allow the existing models to be further
refined and calibrated.

It is intended that this work be used as a reference
and guide when conducting terminal requirements
studies. Depending upon the situation, further
assistance of a consulting nature may be required.
Clearly, without the appropriate background and
understanding of the tools required, it will not be
possible to sit down and apply all the results. But
this is always the case. We would not expect a bank
manager to be able to construct the bank. We would
however, expect her to be able to put together the
team or individuals to accomplish this task, and she
should be able to understand what is needed. As such,
this should also point out what requirements are
needed to quantify the terminal requirements problem.

The book is organized into five chapters. Chapter 1
is an introduction and states the objectives, scope,
and background, and presents the basic problem
structure. This chapter should be read by anyone
interested in or responsible for an online system.
For those interested only in an outline and guide to
the method of analyzing terminal requirements, Chapter
5 gives guidelines to conduct such a study.
References to details in the other chapters are also
made in that chapter.

Chapter 2 covers data collection, Chapter 3 is
concerned with the application of probability theory
to model or represent the observed patterns of
terminal use, and Chapter 4 presents results of
applying these models to real data collected on
terminal use patterns. Chapter 3 contains analytical
methodologies and may be skipped or skimmed by those
not mathematically oriented. It will be valuable to
those interested in the theory and background and
should lend insight into the problem solution and in
turn provide a better feel for what is happening.

Finally, this is an attempt to put together in one
location the required methodologies and show their use
to determine the required number of terminals. If it
is used well, it should generate more data and
expanded models that will aid in determining terminal
requirements.

Acknowledgments

The author acknowledges the National Science
Foundation and OCLC, Inc., which provided the support
necessary to conduct the research which led to this
monograph. Individuals directly involved in the
research were Walter Johnson, Seh-Chang Hah, and
Robert Allison, currently Research Assistants in the
Office of Research at OCLC. Their contributions with
data reduction, programming, and discussions of the
problems were extremely valuable and are greatly
appreciated. In addition, individuals involved in the
data collection activities were Dwayne Ball, Pat
Hartsell, and Joe Harvath, all former Research
Assistants in the Office of Research.

During the course of the research, numerous
individuals contributed both directly and indirectly
to the effort. These include Dr. W. David Penniman,
Vice President of Planning and Research, OCLC. Dr.
Neal Kaske encouraged and supported the writing of
this monograph and provided the opportunity to conduct
the original research. Dr. Michael McGill served as
Project Monitor for the National Science Foundation
and also encouraged this work.

The author also wishes to thank Dr. William J. Studer,
Director of the Ohio State University Libraries and
Susan Logan, Assistant Professor and Coordinator of
Automated Library Services, Ohio State University, and
their staff for providing assistance in obtaining the

data. Such research could not have been completed without their cooperation.

Cindy Heffelfinger and Mary Taylor of the Office of Research, OCLC, were invaluable in their day to day cooperation and assistance. Adrienne Young served as editor. Rick Limes and Richard Skopin were responsible for the graphics. W. David Penniman, Vice President of Planning and Research, Howard Turtle, Senior Research Scientist, Siegfried Dierk, Manager of Documentation Department, and Lois Yoakam, Manager of User Publications Section reviewed the manuscript.

I sincerely thank these individuals and their staff for their efforts and assistance.

Introduction

1.1 Objectives

Research on terminal use was undertaken to produce
management guidelines for libraries to use to predict
the number of public access terminals needed when
automating their catalogs. If the "method" of
purchasing terminals until the money runs out is used,
then research is neither required nor applied. But if
the "method" of optimizing the library's facilities
with respect to both benefits and costs is considered,
then the results of this research should be of
interest.

The question of how many terminals are needed turns
out to be relatively complex. It requires definition
of the library system under consideration, the
constraints involved, and the level of service that
the management chooses to provide.

The results of this research should benefit individual
libraries, library systems, and library networks in
their economic and system planning process. The input
to the budget planning process should more than pay
for the expense of conducting such a terminal–use
study for a specific library. The costs involved in
capital expenses for terminals and monthly costs are
significant; since funding is increasingly difficult
to obtain, potential savings are increasingly
important.

Funding requests demand accurate, quantitative estimates of terminal requirements based on sound data and procedure. The procedures presented here for estimating the required number of terminals, then, should be of particular interest to various levels of the library system.

A large data collection effort was conducted which resulted in observed statistics concerning library traffic behavior patterns of use and demand, the development of measurement procedures and analytical techniques for system evaluation, and the testing of the methodologies with the collected data.

Immediate benefits of this research are the extensive body of data collected and the analysis methodology. Extensive probability model development and testing of observed library patterns for library type and level of service is of particular advantage, as it provides a solid foundation supporting theories both of library demand and of service use patterns, and also makes possible the subsequent application of mathematical queuing models to the library system.

The ultimate benefit, however, is the further application of the methodologies described to the operational analysis of libraries, to answer the terminal requirements question with confidence in the results, but without the necessity of conducting a large-scale research project.

1.2 Scope

The methodology considers several facets of library patron activity in modeling terminal use: catalog use, reference activity, circulation activity, and building occupancy. Predictive models are constructed using regression analysis, stochastic probability distributions of catalog use, queuing analysis for system delay, and sensitivity analysis for consideration of levels of service provided.

Prediction of terminal use is made via regression analysis equations utilizing secondary predictor variables of circulation activity, reference activity, and building occupancy. These three library use factors are attractive for use as predictors because many libraries already collect such data on a regular basis, and it can be economically collected with relative ease. The relationship between these predictor variables and terminal use is described.

Since the distribution patterns of arrivals and service times have been determined through the collected data and the modeling analysis, terminal usage demand is then entered into queuing models to determine the required number of terminals.

1.3 Background

To determine which theoretical models best represent the "real world" situation, data on card catalog use, terminal use, circulation activity, reference activity, and building occupancy was collected at five branches of the Ohio State University Libraries (the Main, Education, Engineering, Undergraduate, and West Campus libraries) over a one-year period covering each of the four academic quarters, from January 1981 through December 1981. From the collected data, the arrival and service patterns were determined, graphed, and analyzed for testing against proposed theoretical models.

The observed distributions were compared with various theoretical models. Two models, the Pearson Type III and the Lognormal distributions, closely matched the data. Regression analysis was performed to determine which of the potential variables of circulation activity, reference activity, and building occupancy were best for predicting terminal and/or card catalog use. Circulation activity (as represented by the number of persons checking out books) was found to be the most reliable predictor of terminal use. Reference activity was found to be another potential predictor, while building occupancy was not reliable.

Parameter estimates for the chosen models were then
developed, and were utilized in queuing analysis
procedures to provide predictions of patron time delay
and number of patrons in the system for various
conditions and levels of service. The results
indicated that sufficient agreement exists between the
theoretical models and the real library data to
confirm the reliability of the models in predicting
the required number of terminals.

1.4   Basic Problem Structure

In any analytical evaluation of an existing system,
certain basic tasks are required to proceed with the
operational analysis:

1. An inventory and evaluation of existing
   operations; and

2. The generation and evaluation of alternative
   improvement schemes considering short-term
   operations and long-term operations.

Given these tasks, a statement of the basic problem
(Task 1) and the solution procedure (Task 2) is
appropriate. In our case, we assume that the patron
demand for library services exceeds the system
capacity (Figures 1-1 and 1-2). As can be observed in
Figure 1-2, when the system demand (library arrival
volume) is greater than the system capacity, a queue
develops. The area between the two curves (Demand and
Capacity) represents the queue, which may be
dissipated over time as system demand drops below
system capacity. The solution to dissipating the
queue may be effected in either of two ways, or a
combination of them: by increasing the system
capacity, or by decreasing the demand on the system.

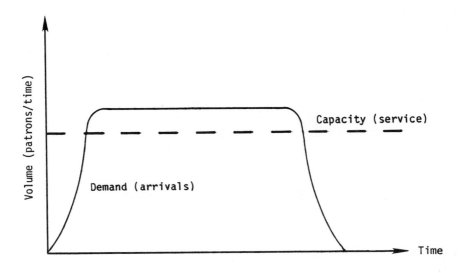

Figure 1-1.   Demand/Capacity Curve Over Time
for Patron Arrivals

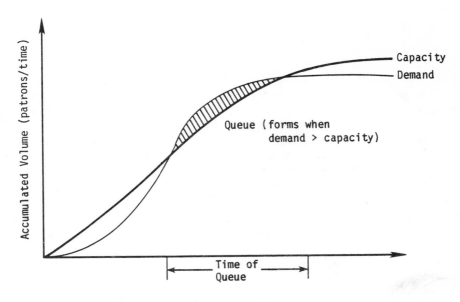

Figure 1-2.   Formation of Queue Over Time
When Demand Exceeds Capacity

The two methods of improving the system so as to avoid generating a queue may be categorized in further detail.

1. Increase system capacity or maintain flow through the system, through

    a. Design (e.g., adding terminals)

    b. Control (e.g., scheduling of terminal use, entrance control, restrict movement of patrons)

    c. Other procedures, such as maintenance scheduling, incident detection (i.e., the detection of malfunctions and trouble spots)

2. Decrease demand on the system

    a. Spread demand over space (e.g., entry control, priority schemes, multiple use schemes)

    b. Spread demand over time (e.g., provide incentives to use the terminals in off-peak hours)

Any analysis must define the desired level of service or "measure of efficiency," which is a function of the demand and capacity, along with the constraints on the system. If the demand on the system is less than the system capacity, the system is considered to be undersaturated. A queue may nevertheless develop due to fluctuations in arrival and service patterns. If the demand exceeds capacity, the system is considered to be oversaturated. In either case, queues will develop, i.e., lines of customers waiting to be served, dependent upon the level of service provided.

One possible approach to determine the number of public access terminals required for a given level of service involves the application of queuing theory, that branch of probabilistic mathematics that deals with the science of delay.

An operational analysis of the library system may be
usefully divided into three complementary tasks:

1. Observed data analysis, including the observed
    statistical analysis of the system;

2. Theoretical development and analysis of the
    system;

3. Queuing and sensitivity analysis of the system.

Obviously, the initial data collection effort provides
the fundamental input to all the analytical tasks;
data collection procedures are discussed in Chapter 2.

Data Collection

The assessment of library use may be based on the
following aspects of patron activity: reference
activity, circulation activity, building occupancy,
and service time at the card catalog or service time
at the terminals (if available).

Data should be collected continuously at the reference
desk, the circulation desk, and at the entrance and
exit gates to determine building occupancy. Service
times at the card catalog and/or terminals need to be
collected only at peak activity times. Two-hour
blocks of time appear to be adequate to obtain a
reading on service time, and the maximum amount of
time that data collectors can make accurate
observations.

The data collection procedures used at The Ohio State
University for this study will be used as an example
to explain the requirements. Such procedures may be
varied depending upon the resources available.

2.1 Locations and Time Periods

Five branch libraries of The Ohio State University
(OSU) were chosen as data collection sites: the Main,
Education, Engineering, Undergraduate, and West Campus
libraries. All five libraries have card catalogs, the
latter four representing only items in that particular

branch, while the Main Library card catalog serves as a union catalog for the OSU Campus System, listing some 3 million volumes. Each library has public access terminals, ranging from 4 terminals in the Engineering Library to 29 in the Main Library. During the summer quarter, the Engineering and West Campus libraries were not included in the study, as the previous year's statistics indicated a level of patron activity too low to justify the time and effort.

Data on circulation desk activity, reference desk activity, and building occupancy was collected by library staff during all hours that the libraries were open (or times that the reference desk was staffed).

Service times at the card catalog and the terminals were collected on a sampling basis. Each data collection shift lasted for two hours and coincided with peak activity times. As determined by statistics collected by library staff for the previous year, the peak activity times occurred three times a day during the week, once on Saturday, and twice on Sunday.

2.2 Training of Collectors

Once the data collection sites had been selected, data collection forms were developed. A form already in use by library staff to record the number of reference and directional queries was used at the reference and circulation desks of each library. The library staff involved in the data collection were not specifically trained, since the procedure was similar to that used to collect HEGIS (Higher Education General Information Survey) information.

The students hired to observe activity at the card catalog and terminals attended an orientation and training session which lasted about an hour and one-half. These sessions, conducted for a maximum of eight students at a time, consisted of a general explanation of the project, a description of the data collection procedures, familiarization with the data collection forms, and a practice session. All

students observed activity at both the card catalog
and terminals.

After the practice session, the students received a
short debriefing which included a review of the time
of their shift, instructions, and names of contacts to
be used if they could not cover their shift. The
students were also given a handbook of data collection
procedures to be reviewed before the collection period
started, and to use as a quick reference. The
handbook is illustrated in Appendix A.

2.3   Data Collection Methodology

2.3.1   Reference Desk and Circulation Desk

Library staff members recorded the number of reference
and directional questions answered at the desks and by
telephone by placing a hash mark in the appropriate
time block on the form after the patron had been
helped. Reference librarians indicated any times that
the reference desk was not staffed by drawing a line
through the appropriate time block. Since the forms
had time blocks representing the weekday hours of the
Main Library, personnel at the branch library
circulation desks also drew lines through those time
blocks during which the branch library was closed.

To minimize imposition on the staff, reference and
directional question data was not collected at the
Main Library's circulation desk, as its reference desk
was almost always staffed during operating hours and
therefore answered most queries. The only
modification made to the libraries' usual procedure
was to collect data in 15-minute segments rather than
on the usual hourly basis. Figure 2-1 illustrates the
form used to record data on activity at the reference
and circulation desks.

LOCATION:_____   DATE:_____

TIME	ON PHONE		TOTAL	TIME	ON PHONE		TOTAL
	REFERENCE	DIRECTIONAL			REFERENCE	DIRECTIONAL	
8:00				3:00			
8:15				3:15			
8:30				3:30			
8:45				3:45			
9:00				4:00			
9:15				4:15			
9:30				4:30			
9:45				4:45			
10:00				5:00			
10:15				5:15			
10:30				5:30			
10:45				5:45			
11:00				6:00			
11:15				6:15			
11:30				6:30			
11:45				6:45			
12:00				7:00			
12:15				7:15			
12:30				7:30			
12:45				7:45			
1:00				8:00			
1:15				8:15			
1:30				8:30			
1:45				8:45			
2:00				9:00			
2:15				9:15			
2:30				9:30			
2:45				9:45			

DIRECTIONS: This sheet is intended as a simple tally of the number of patrons who use the Reference Phone to ask questions of either a reference or directional nature. Please make a tally mark (/) in the appropriate 15 minute box under the appropriate heading after the phone call is terminated.

Please make an X in any time slot during which the reference phone is unattended.

Sheets will be collected at the end of the week.

Figure 2-1. Data Collection Form for Reference and Circulation Activity

2.3.2 Building Occupancy

Building occupancy data was collected by library staff
on an hourly basis, simply by reading counters
attached to each exit and entrance gate. At the Main,
Education, Engineering, and Undergraduate libraries,
gate counters were read on the half-hour to avoid the
increased traffic at change of classes. At the West
Campus library, counters were read on the hour, as
classes changed on the half-hour.

Unfortunately, a number of problems were encountered
in collecting building occupancy data. All five
libraries had counters built into their book security
systems through the exit gates, but only the West
Campus library had an entrance gate counter.
Therefore, entrance gate counters had to be installed
at the other libraries. At the Main Library an
electronic beam crossed the entrance; the counter
would register when the beam was broken. At the
remaining three libraries, counters were attached to
the available turnstiles.

Collecting building occupancy data at the West Campus
library posed no problems except that the counters at
the entrance gate were reset to zero at 5:00 p.m.
every day. The counters at the other libraries had a
variety of problems.

Several times, the counters at the Education Library
short-circuited, as did those at the Undergraduate
Library. At the Engineering Library, the turnstile
was loose so that it would spin if someone hit it
hard, thus registering two or three times as many
bodies as actually went through. One of the counters
at the Main Library would randomly count by one's and
two's; this problem was corrected by the third data
collection period. Thus, only the data on gate counts
from the West Campus library, and that from the Main
Library only for the third and fourth collection
periods is truly reliable. Figure 2-2 illustrates the
form which was used to verify the counters as a check
for reliability of gate counts.

RELIABILITY GATE CHECK

NAME OF LIBRARY: _____   DATE: _____

TIME	ENTRANCE GATES		EXIT GATES	
	GATE A	GATE D	GATE B	GATE C
___:00				
___:15				
___:30				
___:45				
___:00				
___:15				
___:30				
___:45				

Figure 2-2. Data Collection Form for Building
Occupancy (Gate Counts)

2.3.3 Card Catalog

In spaces provided on the data collection form for
arrival and departure times measured by the hour,
minute, and second, data collectors recorded starting
and ending times for each patron that came to use the
card catalog during their shift. Any patrons already
at the catalog before the shift started, or remaining
after the shift ended, were not included in the data
collected for that shift. The data collectors were
supplied with digital watches to record exact arrival
and departure times.

The starting time of a patron's search was defined as
the hour/minute/second that the patron opened a drawer
of the catalog. The end of a search was defined as
the time the patron physically left the card catalog
area, or, in the case of the Main Library, when the
patron left the particular aisle of the catalog.
Leaving the card catalog area was used to define the
end of a search since some patrons use more than a
single drawer for a search and others do not return
drawers to the case after using them. Using the
closing of a card drawer to signal the end of the
search, therefore, often may have been inaccurate.

During the first data collection period (winter
quarter), data collectors were instructed to record
arrival and service times of staff members, as well as
of patrons working in the catalog. Later, if the
collector was not sure whether the catalog user was
staff or patron, the collector was instructed to ask,
time permitting. After the first collection period,
staff were not observed at the catalog, since it was
felt that enough information on staff activities had
been gathered in the first collection period.

Since it was anticipated that a data collector might
have to keep track of a number of people at once,
space was also provided on the data collection form
for user description: immediately obvious
characteristics such as sex, race, and hair color were
used, as well as a brief description of what the
patron was wearing. This information worked well for

collecting card catalog information at the Education,
Engineering, Undergraduate, and West Campus libraries,
since one person observed all catalog activity at each
of those sites.

Because the Main Library catalog was large, the
descriptive information served an additional function:
to trace patrons who used drawers in more than one
aisle during the course of a search. One person could
not monitor every user, so the catalog was divided
into three observation stations, one for each aisle.
One data collector in each aisle recorded arrival and
departure times just for that section of the catalog.
As much information as possible about each patron's
appearance was recorded, as well as notations
indicating if the patron left the aisle and then
returned, and where the patron went.

To obtain complete service times on the 40% of the
users who searched in more than one aisle of the
catalog, a specially trained student assistant
examined all of the Main Library catalog data
collection forms for each shift and collapsed the
entries for those patrons into a single search entry.
Occasionally, patrons disappeared and then reappeared
in the coding sheets. If the disappearance lasted
less than three minutes, the student collapsing the
data treated it as a continuation. If the
disappearance lasted more than three minutes, it was
assumed that the patron had left the catalog area and
then returned. In these circumstances, a second
search entry was recorded. Figure 2-3 illustrates the
form used for gathering card catalog information.

CARD CATALOG USE

DATA COLLECTOR: _____

STARTING TIME: _____ AM PM (circle one)

DATE: _____

LOCATION: _____

AISLE #: _____

SEX M/F	RACE W/B/O	HAIR COLOR	OVER 30 ?	GLASSES ?	UPPER BODY- shirt/sweater/jacket/ etc. (including color)	LOWER BODY- pants/skirt/shorts/ etc. (including color)	ACCESSORIES- backpack/purse/books/ etc. (including color)	STARTING TIME			ENDING TIME			WHERE TO? 1/2/3/T/*
								HOUR	MIN.	SEC.	HOUR	MIN.	SEC.	

Figure 2-3. Data Collection Form for Card Catalog Activity

Because of the potential for error inherent in data
collection at the Main Library with its multiple
observation stations, a reliability check was added to
the procedure. One data collector was routinely
assigned to follow a single patron from start to
finish of a search, regardless of which aisles the
patron travelled through. During the first collection
period, the reliability check was performed by the
data collection supervisor; in subsequent collection
periods, a student was hired for the purpose. If,
however, a shift was shorthanded, the reliability
checker covered one of the regular positions.

2.3.4 Terminals

Gathering data for the terminals was a simpler process
for the observers. Using digital watches, data
collectors recorded only exact starting times, which
were defined as the hour/minute/second that the user
placed his/her hands on the terminal and began to
type.

The observer recorded some descriptive information,
whether the patron got help using the terminal from a
staff member, and which terminal the patron used. To
ensure that the correct terminal number was
identified, signs with large block numbers were placed
on top of each terminal. Figure 2-4 shows the form
used for collecting terminal information.

TERMINAL USE

DATA COLLECTOR:_____   STARTING TIME:_____ A.M.
                                                                         P.M.
                                                                  (circle one)

LOCATION:_____   DATE:_____

TERMINALS BEING OBSERVED: # ___ through # ___ AND # ___ through # ___

TERMINAL I.D. #	STARTING TIME			USER'S SEX	DID USER GET ANY HELP FROM STAFF? (Y/N)	WAS USER A STAFF MEMBER? (Y/N)
	HOUR	MIN.	SEC.			

Figure 2-4. Data Collection Form for Terminal Activity

One collector per library kept track of terminal
activity at the Education, Undergraduate, and West
Campus libraries. Since there are only four public
access terminals at the Engineering Library, it was
possible for the data collector at the card catalog to
monitor the terminals as well.

At the Main Library, 25 of the 29 terminals are
located in the same area. During weekdays and on
Sunday evening, this area was divided into two
observation stations of 12 and 13 terminals watched,
respectively, by two data collectors. Evenings and
weekend afternoons proved to be not as busy as
weekdays, so that one data collector was able to
observe all 25 terminals during these shifts.

The remaining four terminals in the Main Library are
located in the card catalog area. These terminals
were observed by the card catalog data collectors in
the aisle in which the terminals are located. Maps of
all five catalog and terminal data collection sites
are shown in Appendix B.

The observed starting times were then to be matched to
the activity records on computer transaction tapes to
obtain the ending times, and the total search time was
to be calculated during data analysis. However, the
digital watches, which had initially been synchronized
with the internal clock, were found to have "drifted"
over the course of the first three-week data
collection period. Thereafter, the watches were
monitored almost daily by library staff members and
the amount of drift recorded. The difficult process
of determining whether an observed "start time" and a
computer-recorded "stop time" belonged to the same
search was then left to the data analysis phase.
Given the difficulties encountered, it is advisable in
any future studies to determine both start and end
times by the same method, i.e., collect both by
observation or both from the system transaction log.

The interesting phenomenon of "terminal hopping"
(moving from terminal to terminal) was observed early
in the data collection process. Further observation

revealed that this behavior generally occurred
because:

1. The novice user made an error which "locked up"
    the terminal, and simply moved to a new terminal
    rather than spending time correcting the error;

2. The novice user, finding that the system was
    "down" at a particular terminal, and apparently
    believing that it might be "up" at another, tried
    other terminals; or

3. An experienced user, more familiar with one type
    of terminal but finding all those terminals
    occupied began with a less-favored model but moved
    to the familiar terminal when it became available.

Since this behavior did not seem to signal a
continuous search as previously defined for the card
catalog, and was not a frequent occurrence, anyone
physically leaving a terminal and starting again at
another terminal was given a new start time.

In summary, the data collection should be based on the
following aspects of patron activity.

1. Reference, circulation, and building occupancy
    information;

2. Arrivals at the card catalog and terminals;

3. Service times at the card catalog and terminals;

4. The patterns of arrivals and service at the card
    catalog and terminals.

The reference, circulation, and building occupancy
data is required to develop predictive equations for
the arrival rates at the card catalog and terminals.
In turn, knowledge of arrival and service patterns
makes it possible to determine the applicability of
the terminal requirements models as discussed in
Chapter 3.

Application of Probability Theory to Represent Observed Patterns of Terminal Use

The objective of the application of probability theory is to select, refine, and apply mathematical models to describe the patterns, or distributions, of patron flow and use of the online catalog terminals. The models of flow distribution must be specific enough to account for the variance of pertinent parameters, but not so complicated as to make their use impractical in an operating library.

Model application consists of the selection and testing of probability distribution models for predictive power and validity. That is, models are chosen that represent the observed distribution patterns, as well as accommodating a wide range of patron volumes and situational differences in individual libraries. Actual tests of observed distributions versus theoretical distributions consist of both graphic representations and chi-square analysis for "goodness of fit."

3.1 Terminal Use Patterns: Observed Distributions

We wish to have a mathematical model that represents the observed distributions of patron interarrival times and of patron service times when patrons are using the online terminals. Model application first requires data collection and reduction as described in Chapter 2. However, when the applied models reliably

describe what is happening at the terminal areas, they
may be used as a substitute for the expensive and
complicated process of additional data collection. In
addition, the models are used in the queuing analysis,
which is the next step in the methodology, and which
ultimately produces the output of interest, i.e., how
many terminals will be required for the desired level
of service.

3.1.1 Interarrival Patterns

To adequately describe the activity occurring at the
terminals, the observed distribution of arrivals of
patrons approaching the terminals is required.
Interarrival time is defined as the period of time
between the arrivals of one patron and the next. For
example, if the first patron arrives at the catalog
area at 9:04 and the next patron arrives at 9:07:22,
the interarrival time is the difference of arrival
times, or 3 minutes, 22 seconds. Arrival times are
recorded and listed sequentially for the periods of
peak activity, for example, two hours in the morning,
afternoon, and evening.

If these interarrival times are then displayed in a
histogram showing the frequencies of interarrival
times within chosen intervals, the observed
distribution of interarrival times may be presented.
For example, the frequency of arrivals within 30
second intervals may be chosen. This produces the
number of interarrivals between 0 to 30 seconds, 31 to
60 seconds, 61 to 90 seconds, etc., up to the last
interval, which can include all interarrivals past a
chosen time, e.g., 5 minutes. Since an hour is a
universally familiar unit of time, it is convenient to
represent the arrival rate in hourly periods.

At this point, a number of parameters are associated
with each observed interarrival distribution. First,
the number of arrivals per hour is considered to be
the arrival volume. Then, when arrival volume has
been determined, its reciprocal gives the average
interarrival time. For instance, if 15 arrivals occur
during one hour (60 minutes), then the average
interarrival time is 60 minutes/15 or 4 minutes.

3.1.2   Service Patterns

The other distribution that is required to describe
terminal activity is the service time pattern.
Service time is defined as the period of time during
which a patron uses the online catalog, and is
measured from the time that the patron begins using
the terminal to the time terminal use is finished.

The service times are recorded, and plotted in a
histogram showing the frequencies, within chosen time
intervals, of the observed service times at the
terminals; this histogram represents the observed
distribution of service times. Frequencies of service
times may be computed for 30 second intervals or other
selected intervals. For example, the intervals may
display the number of patrons who used the terminal
for 0 to 30 seconds, 31 to 60 seconds, etc., with the
last interval being all service times exceeding a
given period, e.g., 9 minutes.

The service volume is the number of patrons served
during a specific period. When the service volume is
known, then the average service time is easily derived
as the reciprocal of this volume. For example, a
service volume of 9 patrons per hour provides an
average service time of 60 minutes/9 or 6.7 minutes.
Service time is recorded over the same time periods
that arrival times are recorded, so that the observed
service time distributions correspond to the observed
interarrival time distributions.

3.2   Theoretical Probability Distributions

Before attempting to select or test probability
distributions for use as interarrival time and service
time models, one must examine the characteristics of
both the observed and theoretical distributions.
There have been cases in which a theoretical model has
been rejected statistically, while observation of the
graphic data tended to confirm the model's ability to
represent the observed data. The need to match
theoretical models with graphed distributions of

observed data may seem too obvious to mention, but it
is a crucial point.

For example, it would be of little use to attempt to
fit the theoretical distribution called the Pearson
Type I to observed interarrival time data. Since the
Type I distribution is a probability distribution that
is skewed to the right and has its single mode which
is greater than its mean value, it would therefore
tend to assign higher probability to larger
interarrival times. But observed frequency
distributions for patron interarrivals display just
the opposite characteristics, i.e., they are
distributed such that the mode of the distribution is
less than the mean, or skewed to the left. This
indicates that there is a higher probability for the
occurrence of smaller interarrivals or service times.

The question, then, is to consider possible
theoretical probability distributions that represent
the observed distributions. Extensive data
examination leads to the conclusion that the observed
distributions may really be represented by a family of
two probability distribution models. These families
have all the characteristics which are seen in the
observed data. The most promising distributions for
our use are:

> 1. The Pearson Type III distribution
> 2. The Lognormal distribution

Examples of the application of these models may be
found in other fields such as economics, traffic flow
theory, and physics. A brief discussion of these
applicable probability distributions follows.

3.2.1 Pearson Type III Distribution

The Pearson Type III distribution may be stated as
follows for $x \geq 0$:

(1) $f(x) = \dfrac{\lambda^k e^{-\lambda x} x^{k-1}}{\Gamma(k)}$ (probability density function)

where $\Gamma(k)$ = gamma function

(2) $\Gamma(k) = \int_0^\infty x^{k-1}e^{-x}dx$ and $\Gamma(k+1) = k\Gamma(k)$

If we define $\Gamma(k) = (k-1)!$, then for integer values of k, Equation (1) reduces to what is sometimes referred to as the Erlang distribution:

(3) $f(x) = \dfrac{\lambda^k e^{-\lambda x}x^{k-1}}{(k-1)!}$ $; x \geq 0$

Using Equation (3), we may write the distribution function $F(x)$ = Probability that $X < x$ as follows:

(4) $F(x) = P(X < x) = \int_0^x \dfrac{\lambda^k e^{-\lambda x}x^{k-1}dx}{(k-1)!}$

The reduction of $F(x)$ to a simple formula is easily done for integer values of k. For noninteger values of k, it is necessary to evaluate the gamma function with a table or algorithm and use an approximation for the integral.

In the Type III distribution there are two parameters which may be varied, k and λ. Once k is estimated, λ is set to be k/(average interarrival time). Figure 3-1 shows the effect of varying k and holding λ constant.

If $k = 1$, Equation (3) becomes the negative exponential as seen in Figure 3-1. As k increases, the probability density function approaches a normal distribution.

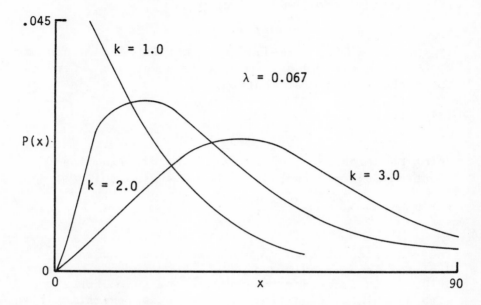

Figure 3-1. Type III Distribution for Various Values of k

Given the Type III distribution, its mean and variance
are:

(5) $E(x) = mean = k/\lambda$
       $Var(x) = k/\lambda^2$

Again for k = 1, the mean and variance reduce to $1/\lambda$
and $1/\lambda^2$ respectively, i.e., the mean and variance of
the negative exponential (note: variance = square of
the mean).

3.2.2 Lognormal Distribution

The lognormal distribution has a variate whose
logarithm follows the normal law of probability.
Consider a random variable X which ranges from zero to
infinity. If we make the transformation Y = lgX,
where lg is the natural logarithm, then Y is again a
random variable having infinite range, $-\infty < X < +\infty$.
If X is normally distributed, then by introducing the
following notation:

(6) $L(x|\mu,\sigma^2) = P(X < x)$ and $N(y|\mu,\sigma^2) = P(Y < y)$

the relation becomes $N(y|\mu,\sigma^2) = N(\lg x|\mu,\sigma^2)$.

That is, L and N are the distribution functions of X and Y, respectively. Because X and Y are related by $L(X) = N(\lg X)$ for $X > 0$,

(7) $L(x) = \int \dfrac{1}{\sigma\sqrt{2\pi}}\, e^{-(\lg t - \mu)^2/2\sigma^2} dt \qquad ; x > 0$

By differentiating L with respect to x, the probability density function of X is obtained as:

(8) $f(x) = \dfrac{1}{x\sigma\sqrt{2\pi}}\, e^{-(\lg x - \mu)^2/2\sigma^2} \quad ; x \geq 0$

Evaluation of this distribution may be carried out via computer using a subroutine or approximation to evaluate the normal distribution. Because Y is normally distributed with mean μ and variance σ^2, $Z = (y-\mu)/\sigma$ has a normal distribution with mean 0, variance 1. As estimates for the parameters,

(9) $\hat{\mu} = \sum\limits_{i=1}^{n} \lg x_i / n$

$\hat{\sigma}^2 = \sum\limits_{i=1}^{n} (\lg x_i - \hat{\mu})^2 / (n-1)$

Figures 3-2, 3-3, and 3-4 show a comparison of the normal probability function and the corresponding lognormal probability function, along with the effect on the lognormal of varying μ and σ^2.

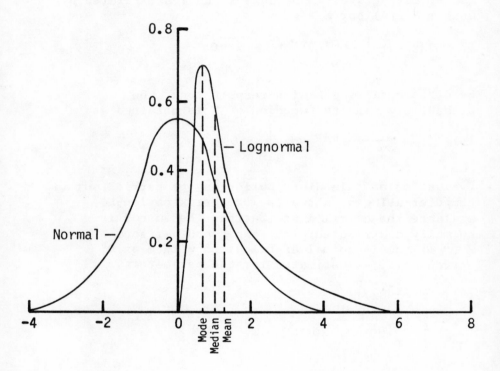

Figure 3-2.   Normal and Lognormal Distributions

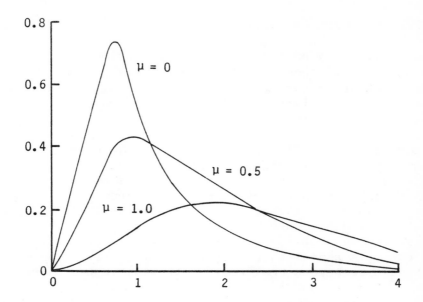

Figure 3-3.   Lognormal Distribution for Different μ

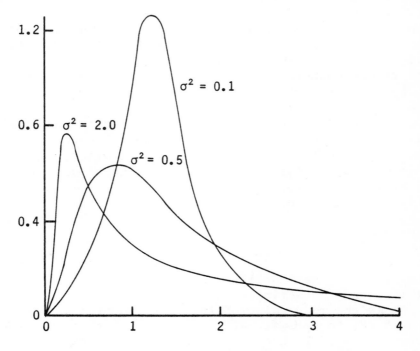

Figure 3-4.   Lognormal Distribution for Different σ^2

3.2.3   Parameter Estimation

The application of theoretical distributions to
observed data, such as patron interarrival time
distribution or service time distribution, requires
that the appropriate functional parameters be
estimated.

The Pearson Type III distribution has two parameters
that require estimation, namely the values of k and λ.
Instead of estimating the value of k, it may be
explicitly chosen by observed data frequency
histograms and consideration of Figure 3-1. If the
distribution seems to be close to random, i.e.,
negative exponential or Poisson arrivals, then k = 1.
If there is a peak to the observed interarrival
frequencies beyond the "zero" interval, then a higher
value of k is chosen, e.g., k = 2. This choice of k,
for libraries, does not seem to go beyond k = 2.

From previous experience, selecting a noninteger value
of k between 1 and 2 is not necessary, as it
complicates the calculations dramatically (using an
integral approximation of the gamma function) and does
little for precision. So the choice is either k = 1
for random patterns or k = 2 for single mode, skewed
to the left behavior.

The second parameter requiring estimation in the Type
III distribution is the value λ. The value of λ turns
out to be equal to 1/(mean value of the distribution).
This result may easily be obtained by using the moment
generating function (mgf) of the Type III
distribution, namely,

$$(10) \quad M_X(t) = \left(\frac{\lambda}{\lambda - t}\right)^k \quad ; \lambda > t \quad \text{(mgf of Type III)}$$

The method of maximum likelihood parameter estimation
will produce an estimate for the theoretical mean,
which is the mean value of the observed frequencies.
Therefore, to estimate λ, use 1/(mean of the observed
frequencies). In the case of k = 1, i.e., negative
exponential, only the mean value of the observed

patron interarrivals is required to be known. This is
obtained as the inverse of the average arrival volume.
For example, if 200 arrivals occur within a 2-hour
period of analysis, then the mean interarrival time is
0.6 minute, i.e., 1/(200 arrivals per 2 hours) =
1/(200/120 minutes) = 120/200 = 0.6 minute.

For parameter estimation in the lognormal
distribution, the same procedure holds, and the
estimates for the parameters (the mean and the
variance) are:

(11) $\overline{X} = \sum_{i=1}^{n} \lg x_i / n$

$V = \sum_{i=1}^{n} (\lg x_i - \overline{X})^2 / (n-1)$

3.3   Testing of Theoretical Vs. Observed Distributions

The testing of theoretical models to fit observed
distributions of interarrival times and service times
should be done in two ways. The most exact method
mathematically is the use of a chi-square analysis,
which is a standard statistical procedure.

To use this method for testing the observed
interarrival distribution for "goodness of fit" to a
theoretical distribution, the observed values of
interarrival frequencies, O_i, are tested against the
corresponding theoretical frequencies, e_i. The
appropriate theoretical parameters, that is, the
distribution mean and variance, may be estimated by
the sample mean and variance as indicated in Section
3.2.3. The calculated chi-square value may then be
compared with the theoretical chi-square value in a
standard statistical chi-square table for a chosen
significance level to test the fit.

In addition to this rigorous mathematical testing of
"goodness of fit," the observed graphic plot should be
compared with the graphic plot of the theoretical
curve. Such a comparison may show that, with the

exception of a few observed values that are out of
bounds, the theoretical distribution is indeed a good
predictor. At such point, judgment should be used to
determine whether the distribution model is a reliable
representative of the patterns observed.

3.4   Regression Analysis to Predict Arrival and Service Demand

We have up to this point explained the methodology
employed, and developed equations where necessary, to
apply to the terminal requirements problem. The
collection of observed terminal use data provides a
straightforward method to obtain the required
information as input to the interarrival models for a
library wishing to replicate the study for its own
purposes. However, libraries currently without online
catalog terminals will also need to determine terminal
requirements. How do they obtain data on service time
distributions?

Obviously, a library may assume conditions comparable
with those studied and select a service volume. This
volume may or may not be representative of that
library's actual conditions. The library may then
proceed to perform an analysis for a range of volumes
and conduct a "sensitivity analysis" on the possible
number of terminals required for different conditions,
e.g., a traffic intensity ranging from 0.6 to 0.99.

It would, however, be advantageous from a number of
points of view to be able to predict the number of
patrons that would use the terminal facilities. Such
a predictive model can be based on the technique of
regression analysis, a brief example being Equation
(12):

(12) $Y = m_1x_1 + m_2x_2 + m_3x_3 + \cdots + m_nx_n + a$

where $x_1, x_2, x_3, \cdots, x_n$ are "independent" predictor
variables; $m_1, m_2, \cdots, m_n, a$ are constants; and Y
represents the dependent variable to be predicted, in
this case, terminal usage. Potential choices for the

"independent" variables $x_1, x_2, \cdots, x_n$ should focus
on those variables which are easily measured and, for
the most part, already routinely collected by
libraries.

It should be emphasized that it is the technique of
collection that is important, not the specific
variables collected. Thus, if a library has other
variables that will satisfy the predictive model, they
may be employed instead. In choosing potential
predictor variables, concentration is on those
variables which will provide information on three
types of activities: circulation desk activity,
reference desk activity, and building occupancy.

Further breakdown of these activities may include, but
not be limited to:

1. Card catalog arrivals
2. Number of books checked out per data collection
   period
3. Number of persons checking out books per data
   collection period
4. Directional questions at reference desk
5. Directional questions at circulation desk
6. Reference questions at reference desk
7. Reference questions at circulation desk
8. Phone activity at reference desk
9. Phone activity at circulation desk
10. Circulation questions at circulation desk
11. Patron counts into library at entrance/exit gates

As one potential regression equation, consider
Equation (13):

(13) $Y = m_1x_1 + m_2x_2 + m_3x_3 + a$

where x_1 = reference desk activity measure
      x_2 = circulation desk activity measure
      x_3 = gate counts
      a = constant
      Y = terminal usage

The development of such an equation is best understood
by first considering only one independent variable x,
and the dependent variable Y, so that Y = mx + b where
x, b are constants. If we plot x = circulation
activity against observed Y = terminal use, a scatter
diagram as in Figure 3-5 is obtained.

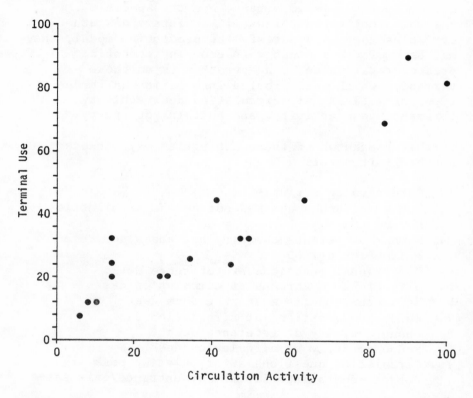

Figure 3-5. Scatter Diagram Showing Observed Terminal
         Use as a Function of Circulation Activity

We may "fit" a linear regression line to these points
(x_1,y_1), (x_2,y_2), $\cdots$, (x_n,y_n) by the method of least squares,
i.e., by minimizing the squares of the deviations of
the linear line through these points, to obtain our
regression equation. In addition, coefficients of
correlation ρ_{xy} may be calculated by using Equation
(14).

(14) ρ_{xy} = correlation coefficient = $\dfrac{E\{[X-E(X)]\ [Y-E(Y)]\}}{\sqrt{\sigma_x^2 \sigma_y^2}}$

where σ_x^2, σ_y^2 = respective variances of x, y

$-1 \leq \rho \leq 1$

The importance of ρ_{xy} is that it is a measure of the association between X and Y. A value of the correlation coefficient near ± 1 indicates a linear relationship. A value near zero only implies the absence of a linear relationship; it does not imply that some other nonlinear relationship may not exist. It is also important to note that, even though we may get a high value of ρ, this only indicates that an association exists, not necessarily a causal relation.

Another useful parameter to be obtained from the regression analysis is the R^2 value. R^2 is a measure of precision for the parameter estimates, where precision is used to describe how well the estimated equation fits the data. R^2 is represented by Equation (15):

(15) $R^2 = \displaystyle\sum_{i=1}^{n} (Y_i - \overline{y})^2 / \sum_{i=1}^{n} (y_i - \overline{y})^2$

where Y_i = calculated Y value
$\overline{y}$ = mean of y_i's
y_i = observed y values

If R^2 is close to 1, most of the variation about the mean is explained by the regression. We then have a satisfactory equation.

The actual multiple linear regressions may be derived for a library or libraries, or for an entire library system; and for various calendar periods, e.g., quarter, entire school year, or smaller segments such as peak use periods. This is a decision that should be made at the library level. The data used in the development of the illustrated regression equations was collected over four quarters, from January 1981 through December 1981, and in five types of academic

libraries. There should be a correlation between the
data collection periods that are used to determine
interarrival distributions and service time
distributions, and the data used to determine
regressions, whenever possible. For example,
regression equations have been developed for each type
of library aggregated over similar academic quarters,
i.e., during the academic year, and separately for
summer quarter. The method of data aggregation will
depend upon observed characteristics, e.g., does the
morning two-hour period of data differ greatly from
that of the afternoon or evening period? Does winter
quarter activity differ from that in the spring
quarter? Does the mean service time vary across
libraries?

3.5 Queuing Analysis

Queuing theory deals with the problem of delay, or
congestion, and the ability to provide adequate
capacity for the average flow through the system.
However, even if the capacity is adequate for the
average flow, delay may occur due to variation in the
flow. The intent of queuing theory is to describe
flow variations and the delays which may occur. The
problem of delay may be considered from either a
spatial or temporal viewpoint, i.e., from the queue
buildup over space (length of queue) or over time
(time spent in the queue).

Given the problem under consideration, one of the
assumptions may be that the patron demand for library
service exceeds the system capacity (Figures 1-1 and
1-2 in Chapter 1). As can be observed in Figure 1-2,
when the system demand (library arrival volume)
exceeds the system capacity (library service ability),
a queue is built up. This queue may then be
dissipated over time, as the system demand again drops
below system capacity. The area between the two
curves (the demand and capacity curves) represents the
queue that has built up. This queue may occur due to
either or both of two factors:

1. A restriction on service, e.g., only a limited number of patrons may be served at a terminal at a time, and the unserved patrons must queue up and await their turn.

2. The service is available during limited time periods; since service is assumed to be available continuously during library hours, this case will not be of interest to us.

The aim of investigating an existing system with congestion is to change the system so as to relieve the congestion problem. If the amount of congestion which occurs due to a series of modifications can be predicted, it is possible to choose the required level of service and design for it. It is also possible to investigate the design and installation of a new system, within given levels of service that are to be provided. Improved service may be achieved in two ways: 1) by increasing the system capacity, or 2) by decreasing the demand on the system.

To conduct the analysis, there are two main properties of the library queuing system which are of interest:

1. The mean and distribution of the length of time a patron is in the queue and the total waiting time where

   total waiting time = queuing time plus service time

2. The mean and distribution of the number of patrons in the system.

Three main characteristics of the library system must be specified in order to perform the analysis:

1. The arrival pattern of patrons, including the arrival rate and distribution of interarrival times, i.e., the time gap between successive arrivals,

2. The service pattern, including the average service time and distribution of service times, and

3. The queue discipline, e.g., first come, first
    served; priority; random service selection, etc.

3.5.1 Single Server, Exponential Interarrivals and Service Times

As an example of the models used, consider a simple
queue with random arrivals and service. Figure 3-6
represents the general concept of a single server
queuing system.

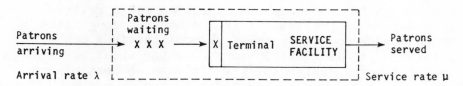

Figure 3-6. Single Server Queuing System

By "random", we mean a specific probability model,
namely, the Poisson arrival pattern with parameter μ
where μ is the average arrival rate. Since we have
assumed random service, this implies that the service
time distribution is negative exponential with
mean = $1/\mu$. Then define:

$$(16) \quad f(x) = \frac{e^{-\mu}\mu^x}{x!} \quad ; x = 0, 1, 2, \ldots$$

and the corresponding Equation (17) as:

$$(17) \quad g(t) = \frac{1}{\mu}e^{-t/\mu} \quad ; t \geq 0$$

To understand the queuing models developed, it is
useful to explain briefly the development of
probability equations to represent queue length and
waiting time. This will serve to define the
terminology used and apply to all the subsequent
models. For purposes of this development, again
assume random arrivals and departures, so that
Equations (16) and (17) are valid. Let

(18) $P_n(t)$ = probability that the system has n patrons at time t,
        i.e., in state n at time t

Now, consider time $(t+\delta t)$. State n may be obtained in time $(t+\delta t)$ in three ways:

i)   The system is in state n at time t and we
        have no arrivals and no departures. The
        probability of this occurrence is:

(19) $P_n(t)[1-\lambda\delta t]\ [1-\mu\delta t] + (\delta t)$
        where λ = arrival rate
              μ = service rate
              t = time interval
              (δt) = probability of 2 or more arrivals or departures in δt
                  where $(\delta t) \to 0$ as $\delta t \to 0$

ii)   The system is in state (n–1) at time t and
        we have one arrival and no departures.
        The probability of this occurrence is:

(20) $P_{n-1}(t)[\lambda\delta t]\ [1-\mu\delta t] + (\delta t)$

iii)   The system is in state (n+1) at time t and we
        have no arrivals and one departure. This
        probability is:

(21) $P_{n+1}(t)[1-\lambda\delta t]\mu\delta t + (\delta t)$

Then our total probability of being in state n at time $(t+\delta t)$ is the sum of these three probabilities:

(22) $P_n(t + \delta t) = p_n(t)(1-\lambda\delta t)(1-\mu\delta t) + p_{n-1}(t)\lambda\delta t(1-\mu\delta t)$

        $+\ p_{n+1}(t)\mu\delta t(1-\lambda\delta t) + (\delta t) \quad\ ; n > 0$

If we then subtract $P_n(t)$ from both sides of Equation (22), divide by δt, and take $\delta t \to 0$, we obtain the set of equations:

(23) $\frac{\partial}{\partial t}P_n(t) = -(\lambda+\mu)p_n(t) + \lambda p_{n-1}(t) + \mu p_{n+1}(t)$

        $\frac{\partial}{\partial t}P_0(t) = -\lambda p_0(t) + \mu p_1(t)$

These may be solved to show that the distribution of
the probabilites p_n is a geometric distribution,
assuming steady-state time independence, so we have:

(24) $P_n = \left(\frac{\lambda}{\mu}\right)^n\left(1-\frac{\lambda}{\mu}\right) = \rho^n(1-\rho)$

> where λ = mean number of arrivals per time interval
> μ = mean number of served patrons per time interval
> ρ = traffic intensity = λ/μ
>   (a measure of system saturation)
> p_n = probability of n patrons in system

The mean of the geometric distribution is given by:

(25) $E(n) = \sum_{n=1}^{\infty} n\rho^n(1-\rho) = \rho/(1-\rho)$

where $E(n)$ = average number of patrons waiting in the
system. Similarly, the variance of the number of
patrons in the system is given by:

(26) $Var(n) = \rho/(1-\rho)^2 = E(n)/(1-\rho)$

We may also show that the probability of a queue
length greater than n in the system is:

(27) $p(\geq n) = \rho^n$

Thus, if ρ is small, large queues are unlikely. Table
3-1 shows an example of the queue length (system)
behavior as ρ varies. If $\rho > 1$, the terms in Equation
(25) are negative. If $\rho = 1$, then Equation (25) is
zero, and we cannot use it. In both cases, the
behavior of the queue is unstable and the formula is
not applicable.

Table 3-1. Example of Queue Length Behavior as
            Traffic Intensity ρ Varies

ρ = traffic intensity	E(n) = mean number in system	Probability of queue ≥ 6
0.10	0.111	0.000
0.20	0.250	0.000
0.30	0.429	0.001
0.40	0.667	0.004
0.50	1.000	0.016
0.60	1.500	0.047
0.70	2.333	0.118
0.80	4.000	0.262
0.90	9.000	0.531
0.95	19.000	0.772

From this table we see that as $\rho \to 0.9$, we have 53% chance of having greater than 5 patrons in the system (in the queue and being served).

If we are interested in the average or expected number of patrons just in the queue and not being served, this can be obtained from the relation in Equation (28):

(28) $E_q(n) = \rho E(n) = \rho^2/(1-\rho)$

In a similar manner, the distribution of waiting times of patrons may be derived. We shall not go through these derivations, but only list a few of the pertinent results that are applicable. Since the service time distribution is negative exponential, the distribution of waiting times turns out to be the sum of k negative exponential distributions, i.e., it is a Pearson Type III distribution:

(29) $w(x|k) = \dfrac{\mu^k e^{-\mu x} x^{k-1}}{\Gamma(k)}$; $x \geq 0$

where $w(x|k)$ = the probability density function for waiting time $\leq x$,
  k = number of patrons, and
  $\mu = k/\bar{t} = k$/average waiting time.

Now, since the probability of a queue of length n is $p_n = (1-\rho)\rho^n$, we have the unconditional distribution of waiting time as:

(30) $w(x) = (1-\rho)\delta(x) + \sum_{k=1}^{\infty} \dfrac{\mu^k e^{-\mu x} x^{k-1}}{\Gamma(k)} (1-\rho)\rho^k$; $\delta(x) = \begin{cases} 0 \text{ if } k > 0 \\ 1 \text{ if } k = 0 \end{cases}$

i.e.,

(31) $w(x) = (1-\rho)\delta(x) + \rho(\mu-\lambda)e^{-\mu x + \lambda x}$

Integrating

(32) $W(x) = \int_0^x w(x)dx = 1 - \rho e^{-\mu(1-\rho)x}$

is the cumulative distribution function, and

(33)   Average waiting time in the queue = $w(x) = \dfrac{\rho}{\mu(1-\rho)}$

(34)   Variance of waiting time in the queue = var $w(x) = \dfrac{\rho(2-\rho)}{\mu^2(1-\rho)^2}$

(35)   Average waiting time in the system = $\dfrac{1}{(\mu-\lambda)}$

A summary of these equations along with some other useful derivations are found in Table 3-2. These results apply to the case of random arrivals and service, i.e., negative exponential interarrival times and service times and a single server.

Table 3-2. A Summary of Queuing Relationships for
Exponential Interarrivals and Service Times
and a Single Server

Spatial Relations

1. P(n) = probability of n patrons in system $P(n) = \rho^n(1-\rho)$
2. E(n) = mean number of patrons in system $E(n) = \rho/(1-\rho)$
3. $E_q(n)$ = mean number of patrons in queue $E_q(n) = \rho^2/(1-\rho)$
4. Var(n) = variance of number of patrons in system $Var(n) = \rho/(1-\rho)^2$

Temporal Relations

5. f(t) = probability of having spent time t in system $f(t) = \rho(\mu-\lambda)e^{(x-\mu)t}$
6. $\overline{W}$ = average time in system $\overline{W} = 1/(\mu-\lambda)$
7. $\overline{W}_q$ = average waiting time in queue $\overline{W}_q = \lambda/[\mu(\mu-\lambda)]$
8. Probability ($\leq$ t) = probability spending $\leq$ t in system $Pr(\leq t) = 1-e^{-(1-\rho)\mu t}$
9. Probability$_q$($\leq$ t) = probability spending $\leq$ t in queue $Pr_q(\leq t) = 1-\rho e^{-(1-\rho)\mu t}$

3.5.2 Multiple Server, Exponential Interarrivals and Service Times

We may carry our queuing analysis further and consider
multiple service channels (terminals). Figure 3-7
represents the general concept of a multiple server
queuing system.

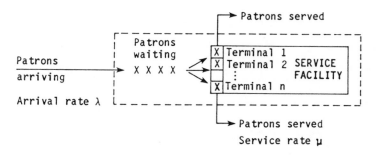

Figure 3-7. Multiple Server Queuing System

If we again assume random arrivals and service times, that the patron moves to the first available terminal for service, and that each terminal has the same service rate, then:

1) The number of patrons in the queue = 0 if n (number of patrons in the system) $\leq$ k (number of terminals).

2) If n > k, see Table 3-3 for corresponding equations.

Table 3-3. Random Arrivals and Service for Multiple Service Stations (Lead Patron Moves to First Vacancy)

Spatial Relations

1. probability of zero patrons in system

$$p(0) = 1 / \left[\sum_{n=0}^{k-1} \frac{1}{n!} (\frac{\lambda}{\mu})^n + \frac{1}{k!} (\frac{\lambda}{\mu})^k \frac{k\mu}{(k\mu-\lambda)} \right]$$

2. probability of n patrons in system for $0 \leq n < k$; k = number of terminals

$$p(n) = \frac{1}{n!} (\frac{\lambda}{\mu})^n p(0)$$

   for $n \geq k$

$$p(n) = \frac{1}{k! k^{n-k}} (\frac{\lambda}{\mu})^n p(0)$$

3. Average number of patrons in system

$$E(n) = \frac{\lambda\mu(\lambda/\mu)^k}{(k-1)! (k\mu-\lambda)^2} p(0) + \frac{\lambda}{\mu}$$

4. Average length of queue

$$E_q(n) = \frac{\lambda\mu(\lambda/\mu)^k}{(k-1)! (k\mu-\lambda)^2} p(0)$$

Temporal Relations

5. Average time in system

$$\overline{w}(t) = \frac{\mu(\lambda/\mu)^k}{(k-1)! (k\mu-\lambda)^2} p(0) + \frac{1}{\mu}$$

6. Average time in queue

$$\overline{w}_q(t) = \frac{\mu(\lambda/\mu)^k}{(k-1)! (k\mu-\lambda)^2} p(0)$$

7. Probability of waiting $\leq$ t in system

$$p(\leq t) = 1-e^{-\mu t} \left[1 + \frac{p(n > k)}{k} \cdot \frac{1-e^{-\mu k t[1-(\lambda/\mu k)-(1/k)]}}{1-(\lambda/\mu k)-(1/k)} \right]$$

8. Probability of having to wait in queue

$$\sum_{n=k}^{\infty} p(n) = (\frac{\lambda}{\mu})^k \frac{p(0)}{k! (1-\lambda/\mu k)}$$

9. Probability waits $\leq$ t in queue

$$P_q(\leq t) = 1-p(k)e^{-(k-\rho)t\mu}$$
where $p(k) = P(n \geq k)$

A specific example may further explain the models. Consider a library with 20 online terminals and an average arrival of 80 patrons between the hours of 10 a.m. and 12 p.m., in a random manner. Measurement shows the terminal service times to be randomly distributed with a mean service time of 10 minutes. The following questions may be addressed:

1. Probability of the terminal area being empty.
2. Average number of patrons being served.
3. Average number of patrons waiting in the queue.
4. Average time spent in the queue.
5. Probability of having to wait two minutes or less in the queue.

To determine the answers to these questions, it is assumed that there are multiple service channels. Then the parameter values become:

λ = 80 patrons/2 hours,
μ = 1 patron/10 minutes = 12 patrons/2-hour period, per terminal,
k = number of terminals = 20.

Assuming multiple service channels, the equations in Table 3-3 apply. The solutions are:

1. p(0) = probability of empty terminal area

   $e^{-\lambda/\mu} = e^{-80/12} = e^{-6.67} \rightarrow 0$

   [This is obtained from equation 1 in Table 3.3. The second part of the denominator goes to zero, while the first part is just the series representation of the exponential function.]

2. E(n) = λ/μ = 6.67

   [since p(0) $\rightarrow$ 0]

3. $E_q(n)$ = E(n) - λ/μ = 0

4. $\overline{w}_q$ = 0

5. Prob (t $\leq$ 2 min) = 1 - $e^{-(1/12)\,(1/60)}$ $\rightarrow$ 1

Looking at these results we conclude:

1. It is unlikely that we will have an empty terminal
   area, since such probability approaches zero.

2. The average number of patrons being served is 7
   (rounding 6.67 off to 7).

3. The average number of patrons waiting in the queue
   is zero.

4. The average time spent in the queue approaches
   zero.

5. The likelihood of waiting less than 2 minutes is
   nearly 100%, i.e., the probability goes to 1.

3.5.3 Other Potential Models

At this point it is appropriate to make some
statements concerning assumptions and other possible
queuing patterns which may apply to library service.
Although it is not necessary to use all the models
referred to, it is important to be aware of some of
the underlying assumptions and constraints. Specific
comments or assumptions are:

1. We have assumed steady-state conditions, at least
   for the analysis time period.

2. The traffic intensity $\rho = \lambda/\mu$, i.e., the ratio of
   arrival rate to service rate is < 1.

3. Type of service is first come, first served,
   single service or multiple service channels.

4. Negative exponential interarrivals and service
   times.

5. System includes patrons waiting to be served plus
   those being served.

6. If the service rate μ is less than the arrival
    rate λ, i.e., $\rho \geq 1$, then we have a time-dependent
    system where demand is greater than capacity.
    Then the average number of patrons in the system
    $E(q(t))$ at time t after the the peak starts is
    given by the number in the system before the peak
    plus the number of arrivals and minus the number
    of departures in time t, i.e.,

(36) $E(q(t)) = E(q) + \lambda t - \mu t$

A few general cases will be given at this point
without detail development. Assuming we have random
interarrivals, and unspecified service pattern, then

(37) $E_q(n)$ = number of patrons in the queue = $\rho + \dfrac{\rho^2(1+C^2)}{2(1-\rho)}$

where C = coefficient of variation of the service time
distribution, i.e.,
C = standard deviation/mean.

For example, if we have random service, with mean
value $1/\lambda$, then the variance is $1/\lambda^2$,

and $C = (1/\lambda)/(1/\lambda) = 1$

and $E(n) = \rho/(1-\rho)$

which is the same result as before.

An interesting thing occurs if we are able to hold the
service constant. If the service times are constant,
then this implies zero variance or standard deviation.
Thus C = 0 and our equation for the average number of
patrons in the queue becomes:

(38) $E_q(n)$ = constant service = $\dfrac{\rho(1-\frac{1}{2}\rho)}{(1-\rho)}$

Now, taking the ratio of constant to random expected
patrons in the queue, we have $\dfrac{E_q \text{ (constant)}}{E_q \text{ (random)}} = 1-\frac{1}{2}\rho$

If ρ is small, there is very little reduction in
average queue size if we change from random to regular

service, but as $\rho \rightarrow 1$, the reduction in average queue size approaches 50%.

The conclusion from this theoretical analysis is that the average queue size may be cut in half by introducing regular service times. Whether this is practical under real conditions is another question. There are situations where this is applicable and feasible, such as tunnel facilities in road traffic flow. The Lincoln Tunnel between New York and New Jersey is an example of a successfully implemented regulated-flow system. The intent behind introducing a regular service pattern rather than a random one is to reduce the fluctuations in flow, thus more effectively dampening any disturbances in flow that may occur, and preventing the formation of large queues.

4

Terminal Use Patterns and the Required Number of Terminals to Satisfy Demand: Results

To confirm the reliability of the potential
theoretical distribution models and the corresponding
queuing models, it was necessary to determine patterns
of library use from observed data for comparison.
Such patterns were extensively examined in data
collected at The Ohio State University for the entire
year of 1981. Obtaining data at five different branch
libraries for each of the four academic quarters made
it possible to distinguish differences in
characteristics by library type and by time of year.

4.1 Distribution of Interarrivals

Observed frequency histograms were constructed for
interarrivals for each of the five libraries and for
each of the four academic quarters. For each library,
observed distributions were made for both the card
catalog and the terminals; for the Main Library,
arrivals were also determined at the circulation desk.

In some cases, the histograms were constructed over
different interval sizes. In most cases, however,
30-second intervals were chosen, so that frequencies
were determined for (0,30), (30,60), (60,90), ••• ,
(t-30,t), ••• , (t,∞), the last interval consisting of
all interarrivals > t seconds. Figures 4-1 through
4-40 show these interarrival histograms along with
mean interarrival times.

Figures 4-41 through 4-44 chart the mean interarrival
times at all the libraries for each academic quarter.
These charts illustrate that the Main Library
generally had the lowest mean interarrival time while
the Undergraduate Library generally had the highest
mean interarrival time.

We may also observe the variance in each library's
mean interarrival time across quarters, as seen in
Figures 4-45 through 4-49. Tables 4-1 through 4-4
consist of a summary of the observed distribution
statistics, including mean arrival times, the
theoretical model most appropriate, parameter estimate
values, and sample volume.

After being compared with the observed frequency
histograms for interarrivals, the theoretical models
were used to generate theoretical distributions for
each library and each quarter, at both card catalog
and terminal locations. These models were tested in
two ways: 1) by simply observing the "fit" of the
theoretical curve to the observed data, and 2) by
using a chi-square "goodness of fit" test.

Three separate models were tested: the Pearson Type
III with $k = 1$ (negative exponential), the Pearson
Type III with $k = 2$, and the Lognormal. Table 4-5
contains the results of these analyses. The analyses
indicate that in basically all the cases, the most
appropriate model for interarrival distribution is the
negative exponential (Pearson Type III, $k = 1$), i.e.,
"random" behavior of arrivals.

4.2 Distribution of Service Times

Observed frequency histograms were also constructed
for service times at both the card catalog and the
terminals for each of the libraries and across
quarters. Figures 4-50 through 4-93 show the results
along with the theoretical distribution curves.
Figures 4-94 through 4-98 show the mean service times
over quarters by library, while Figures 4-99 through
4-102 illustrate the mean service times over libraries
by quarter.

These charts show that card catalog mean service times
are always less than the corresponding terminal mean
service times (for a given library and quarter). The
range of mean service times is 2.41 minutes at the
Undergraduate Library to 6.82 minutes at the Main
Library for the card catalog. The range of mean
service times is 4.95 minutes at the Engineering
Library to 9.75 minutes at the West Campus Library for
terminals. This clearly shows a difference among
libraries at the same institution.

In the majority of situations, service patterns may be
represented by the negative exponential distribution.
However, there are some cases in which the lognormal
distribution represents a better model for service
time. There is a tendency for service times to
increase to a peak and then fall off in frequency as
they increase. Tables 4-6 through 4-9 summarize the
observed and theoretical service patterns, while Table
4-10 contains the results over quarters including test
results and mean service times.

The results of the model testing are encouraging from
two points of view. The first is that it is always
encouraging just to be able to accurately model and/or
predict the behavior of a "human dependent" system and
have confidence in the models. The second encouraging
point is that it is possible to create manageable
queuing models for either single station or multiple
station situations that can be analyzed via computer.
Although admittedly the formulae presented in Chapter
3 may seem formidable, they are manageable compared
with other possible situations.

4.3 Regression Analysis

Regression analysis is used to provide the capability
to predict potential terminal usage, i.e., terminal
arrivals. For a system that is already operational,
terminal arrival volume may be measured directly, as
well as mean service times. But when dealing with a
nonexistent system, how does one know future terminal
usage? Regression analysis provides a method to

predict terminal use as a function of predictive
variables dealing with circulation activity, reference
activity, and building occupancy (or gate counts).
These are measures that are normally obtained at a
library and if not, they may be easily obtained.

There is one point to keep in mind: any regression
analysis in reality only applies to the situation
where the data was collected. The application of the
models to other situations may be expected to be valid
in proportion to the likeness of the situations. That
is, a comparison of libraries A and B, which are the
same type of library, at the same institution during
similar time periods should be the same. But a
comparison of library C, of a different type at a
different institution during a different time period
may not be valid.

A possible way around this is to develop regression
equations for the applicable library to predict card
catalog use. At this stage one may use a relationship
between card catalog use and terminal use for a
similar situation where both card catalogs and
terminals are in existence. However, the important
points are to recognize the limitations of
applicability and to attempt to define similar
systems.

In the case where terminals are not available or the
library is designing for future demand levels,
regression equations may be utilized to predict
terminal demand. After obtaining scatter diagrams as
shown in Chapter 3, the method of least squares
analysis was used to develop the corresponding
multiple regression equations. Equations were
developed for each library as well as a general
equation encompassing the entire set of data from all
the libraries. Terminal usage was considered as a
function of books checked out and then as a function
of the number of persons checking out books as
represented by Equation (39).

(39) $Y = mx+b$

     where x = number of persons checking out books
          y = terminal usage
          m and b are regression constants

Table 4-11 summarizes how certain variables predict terminal arrivals. It is suggested that regression equations be developed for the appropriate library systems, if feasible, with the staff and skills available. Such equations should consider the following variables as potential predictors of terminal use: circulation activity, reference activity, and building occupancy.

The analysis conducted on the Ohio State University Libraries data indicates that terminal usage is most closely correlated with circulation activity (number of people checking out books), as compared with correlation with reference desk activity (questions asked at the reference desk) or building occupancy (gate counts). In particular, the R^2 measure for regression of terminal usage for all libraries and the resulting regression equations on these measures are as follows.

Terminal usage (Y) regressed on number of persons checking out books:

   $R^2 = 0.667$ Sample size = 801
   $Y = 1.23X + 11.53$

Terminal usage (Y) regressed on reference desk activity (X = sum of all three questions asked at reference desk):

   $R^2 = 0.454$ Sample size = 384

   $Y = 0.84X + 23.13$

Terminal usage (Y) regressed on building occupancy (X = gate counts):

   $R^2 = 0.331$ Sample size = 108

   $Y = 0.08X + 16.11$

This analysis may be taken a step further by
calculating the regression of terminal usage on all
three of the above independent variables at the same
time. This produces terminal usage regressed on
persons checking out books, reference activity, and
gate counts. The results are not adequate, showing
little correlation and also based on a small
comparative sample size of 108 (as compared with a
sample size of 801 for persons checking out books).

Therefore, it is not recommended to use all three of
these variables as predictors. Better results are
obtained utilizing only circulation activity as a
predictor. Corresponding regression equations for the
individual libraries have also been developed. In
most cases, the R^2 values are lower than those
obtained in aggregating the libraries and then
obtaining the regression. For this reason, it is
recommended that data be aggregated over all library
types and also be compared with the equations obtained
from individual libraries regressed over the
independent variables, if new regression equations are
developed at the local library level.

Now suppose terminals are in existence at the library
system under consideration. In this case, the
regression may be terminal usage on card catalog
usage. This produced an overall regression equation
and R^2 value as follows.

$R^2 = 0.720$ Sample size = 777

$Y = 0.97X + 10.31$

A further refinement to include books checked out,
card catalog use, and persons checking out books
produced:

$R^2 = 0.718$ Sample size = 716

$Y = 0.10X_1 + 0.55X_2 + 0.40X_3 + 8.26$

X_1 = books checked out

X_2 = card catalog use

X_3 = persons checking out books

Y = terminal use

The output of the chosen regression equation will
serve as input to the queuing models, i.e., the
arrival rate λ. The required service rate may be
obtained from the mean service times. If the
terminals are already present, mean service times may
be determined from direct observation. At this stage,
the arrival and service distributions have been
determined along with values for the required
parameters. The remaining task consists of inputting
this information into the queuing models and
determining the required number of terminals for the
chosen levels of service.

4.4   Queuing Models to Predict the Required Number of Terminals

The application of the queuing models from Chapter 3
may now be used to illustrate the method of terminal
prediction. Suppose that the system under
consideration is a multiple-server queue with Type III
distribution, k = 1 (negative exponential)
interarrivals and service patterns, and the queue
discipline is first come, first served. This fully
specifies the system by describing the three necessary
elements of:

i)   arrival pattern: the average rate of arrival of
      patrons and the interarrival distribution
      function.

ii)   service pattern: the description of how service
      takes place, i.e., the average service rate at
      the terminals and the service distribution
      function.

iii) queue discipline: the method of selecting a
      patron for service from those waiting to be
      served, e.g., first come, first served.

Then the equations within Chapter 3 are applicable.
To simplify the use of these queuing relationships, a
number of nomograms have been developed as shown in
Tables 4-12 through 4-14 and in Figure 4-103. These

are based on standard tables which calculate the
values of exponential functions.

Consider the following example in using these
nomograms. We will use the notation previously
introduced in Chapter 3. To generate the required
number of terminals, certain assumptions and
constraints must be applied. Let λ be the mean
arrival rate (per time unit) of patrons, μ be the mean
service time per terminal. Further, let t be the
maximum acceptable time allowed for waiting in a
queue, and k represent the number of terminals
provided. Then the waiting time in the queue is
represented by:

(40) $P(\text{waiting} < t) = 1 - P_k \cdot e^{-(k-\rho)t\mu}$

We will use this equation to calculate the number of
terminals required to satisfy our demand within given
constraints. An example will be useful to demonstrate
this application.

Suppose measurement shows patron arrivals to be 600
per hour and similarly the mean service time to be 30
seconds. If the terminal design criteria is to assure
that 90% of the patrons do not wait more than one
minute, then we may set up our equation as follows:

(41) $P(\text{waiting} < 60 \text{ seconds}) = 0.90$

and solve this equation for k. Substituting into
Equation 40, we have:

(42) $P(< 60 \text{ sec}) = 1 - P_k \cdot e^{-(k-\rho)t\mu} = 0.90$

         i.e., $1 - P_k \cdot e^{-(k-\rho)t\mu} = 0.90$

         but t = 60 sec, λ = 600 patrons/hr = 10 patrons/min
         $\mu = 1/(30 \text{ sec/patron}) = 1/(½ \text{ min/patron}) = 2 \text{ patrons/min}$
         $\rho = \lambda/\mu = 10/2 = 5$

Then,

(43) $1 - P_k \cdot e^{-(k-5) \cdot 60/30} = 0.90$

         i.e., $1 - P_k \cdot e^{-(k-5) \cdot 2} = 0.90$

The solution may be obtained by substituting values of k. In order to make this more usable, tables may be constructed, such as shown in Table 4-12. To use this table, first determine the value for $t\mu$, which in our case is 60 x (1/30) = 2 (being careful to always deal in the same time units, i.e., if seconds are used for waiting time, service rate should be in units of 1 patron served per mean service time). Then finding $t\mu$ = 2.0 across the top of the table, we proceed down the column until the appropriate value for $\lambda/\mu = \rho$ = trafic intensity = 5 is found. In our case, we find ρ = 5.08. Proceeding back across the row to the appropriate k value, shows k = 6. That is, 6 terminals will satisfy this demand 90% of the time.

If we proceed to Table 4-13, which represents the number of terminals required to satisfy 95% of the demand, we find an increase to 7 terminals. Table 4-14 represents a 99% probability of waiting in the queue.

Figure 4-103 is a nomogram showing the probability of waiting within a queue, i.e., the probability that all k terminals are in use. For k = 1, this is simply ρ = λ/μ = utilization. Along the top of Figure 4-103, k = number of servers is plotted from k = 1 to k = 100; P($\geq$k) is represented by the vertical axis and traffic intensity ρ = λ/μ is along the horizontal axis.

To use this nomogram, first calculate the traffic intensity, e.g., 5 with 6 terminals from the preceding example. Then let the probability that an arriving patron must wait with 2 patrons within the system be P($\geq$6). Using Figure 4-103, locate a traffic intensity of ρ = 5 along the horizontal axis and proceed vertically until crossing the k = 6 terminals curve. From here proceed to the left vertical axis and read the probability P(>6) = 0.58. That is, there is a 58% chance of waiting in the queue. The addition of another terminal lowers this to 0.36.

FIGURES 4-1 TO 4-40
OBSERVED VS. THEORETICAL DISTRIBUTIONS: INTERARRIVALS

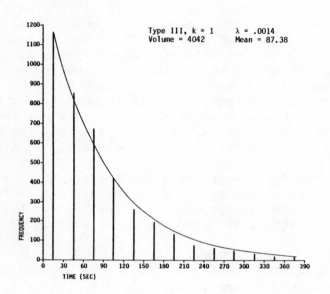

Figure 4-1.   Main Library
Card Catalog - Winter 1981

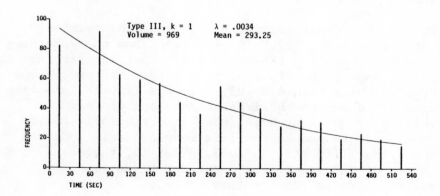

Figure 4-2.   Main Library
Terminals (Card Catalog) - Winter 1981

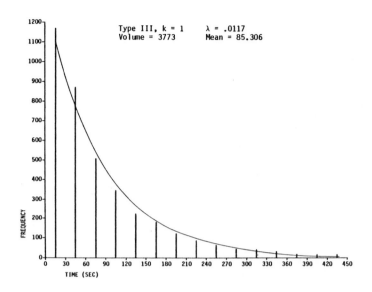

Figure 4-3.   Main Library
Terminals (Circulation Desk) - Winter 1981

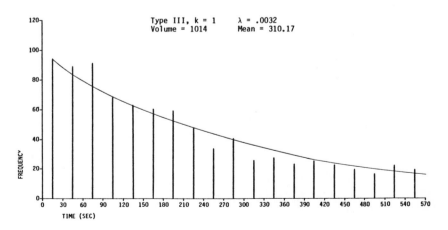

Figure 4-4.   Education Library
Card Catalog - Winter 1981

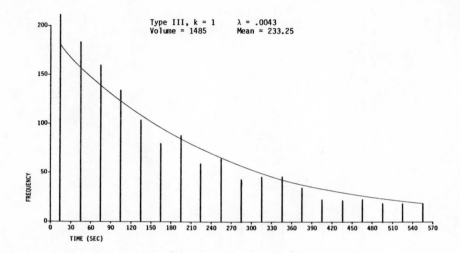

Figure 4-5.   Education Library
Terminals — Winter 1981

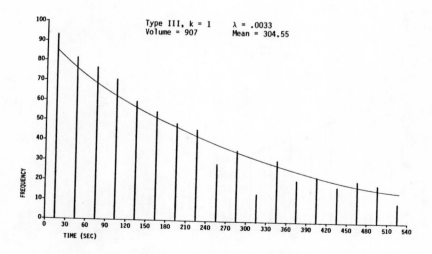

Figure 4-6.   Engineering Library
Card Catalog — Winter 1981

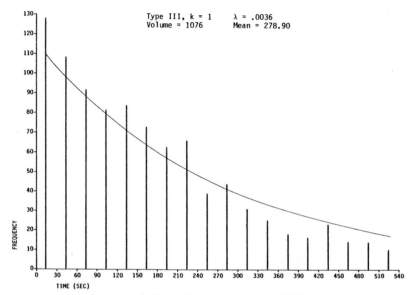

Figure 4-7. Engineering Library
Terminals — Winter 1981

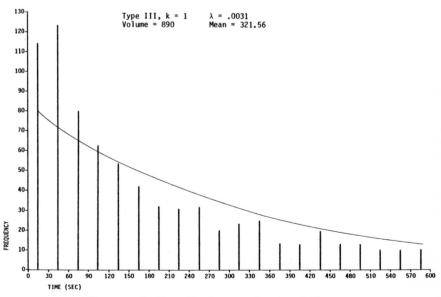

Figure 4-8. Undergraduate Library
Card Catalog — Winter 1981

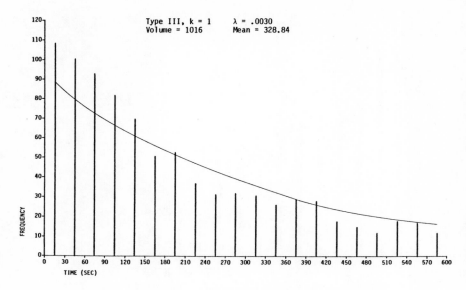

Figure 4-9.   Undergraduate Library
Terminals – Winter 1981

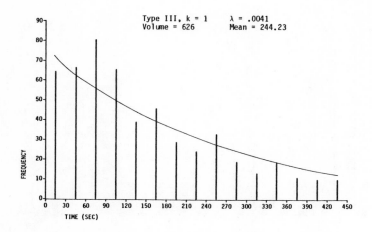

Figure 4-10.   West Campus Library
Card Catalog – Winter 1981

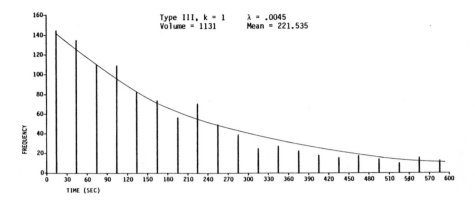

Figure 4-11.   West Campus Library
Terminals – Winter 1981

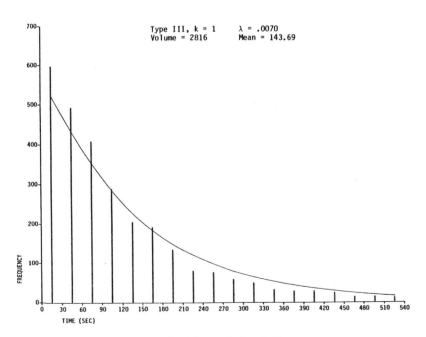

Figure 4-12.   Main Library
Card Catalog – Spring 1981

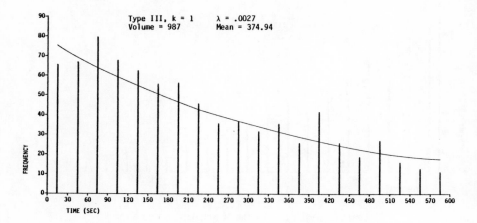

Figure 4-13. Main Library
Terminals (Card Catalog) — Spring 1981

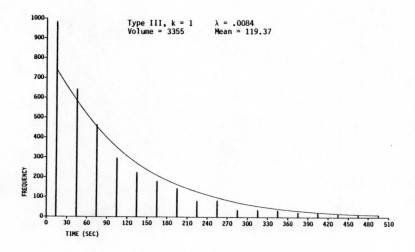

Figure 4-14. Main Library
Terminals (Circulation Desk) — Spring 1981

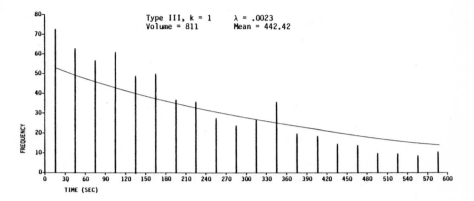

Figure 4-15.   Education Library
Card Catalog — Spring 1981

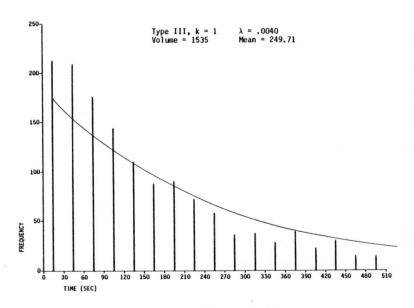

Figure 4-16.   Education Library
Terminals — Spring 1981

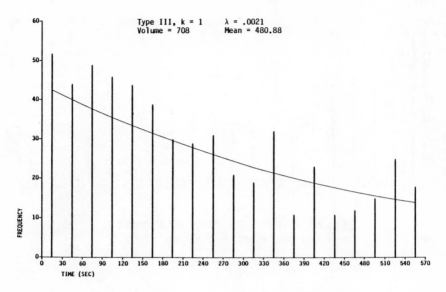

Figure 4-17. Engineering Library
Card Catalog — Spring 1981

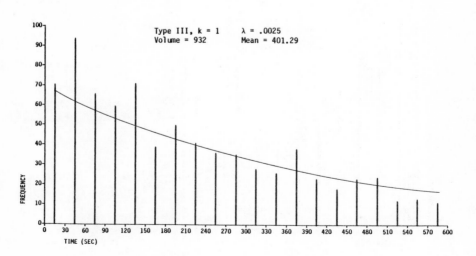

Figure 4-18. Engineering Library
Terminals — Spring 1981

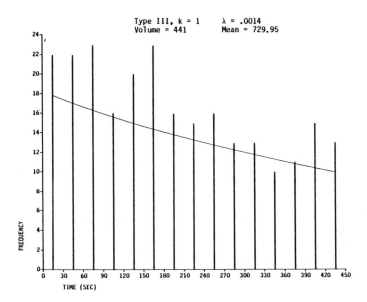

Figure 4-19. Undergraduate Library
Card Catalog — Spring 1981

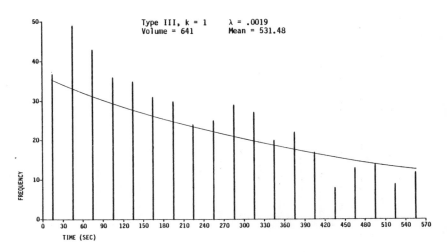

Figure 4-20. Undergraduate Library
Terminals — Spring 1981

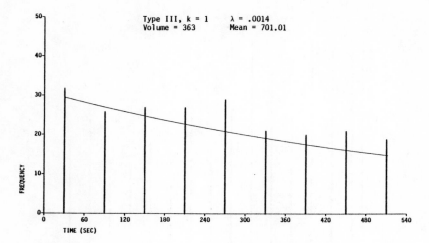

Figure 4-21.   West Campus Library
Card Catalog — Spring 1981

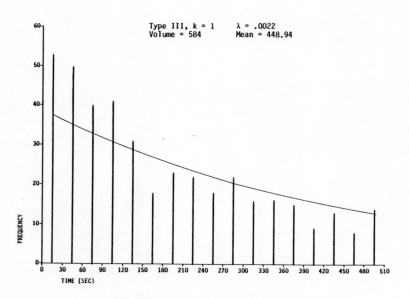

Figure 4-22.   West Campus Library
Terminals — Spring 1981

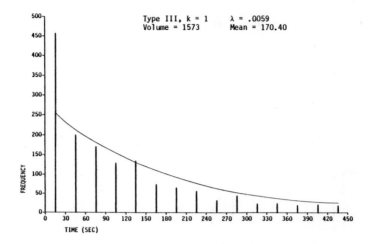

Figure 4-23.   Main Library
Card Catalog - Summer 1981

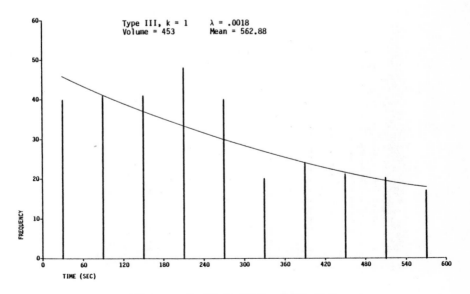

Figure 4-24.   Main Library
Terminals (Card Catalog) - Summer 1981

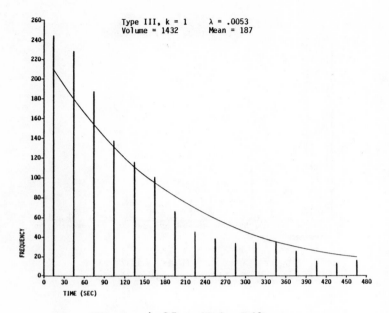

Figure 4-25. Main Library
Terminals (Circulation Desk) - Summer 1981

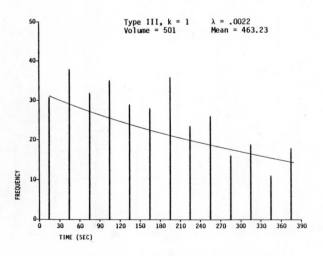

Figure 4-26. Education Library
Card Catalog - Summer 1981

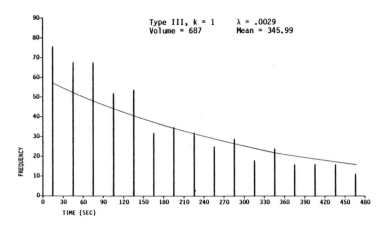

Figure 4-27. Education Library
Terminals – Summer 1981

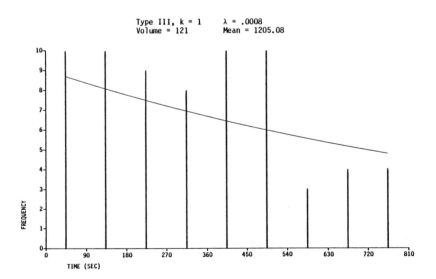

Figure 4-28. Undergraduate Library
Card Catalog – Summer 1981

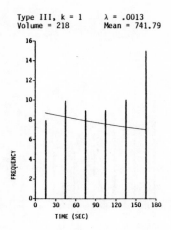

Figure 4-29.   Undergraduate Library
Terminals — Summer 1981

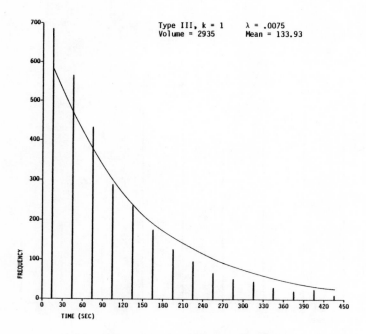

Figure 4-30.   Main Library
Card Catalog — Fall 1981

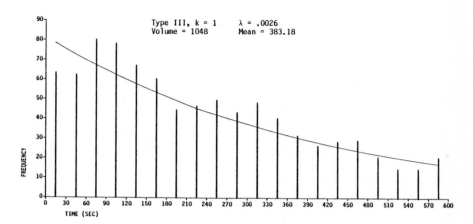

Figure 4-31. Main Library
Terminals (Card Catalog) - Fall 1981

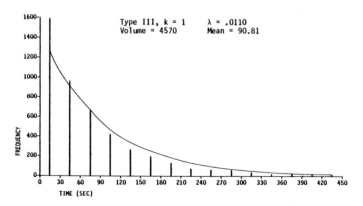

Figure 4-32. Main Library
Terminals (Circulation Desk) - Fall 1981

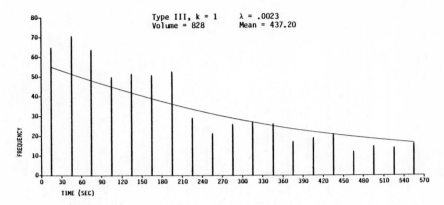

Figure 4-33.   Education Library
Card Catalog – Fall 1981

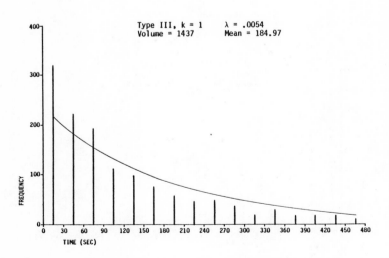

Figure 4-34.   Education Library
Terminals – Fall 1981

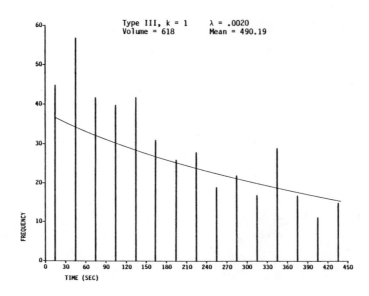

Figure 4-35. Engineering Library
Card Catalog - Fall 1981

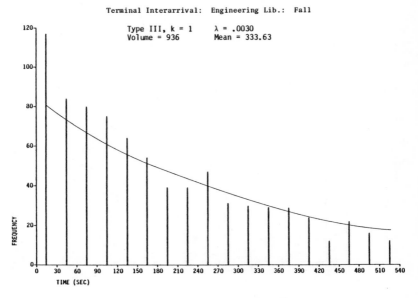

Figure 4-36. Engineering Library
Terminals - Fall 1981

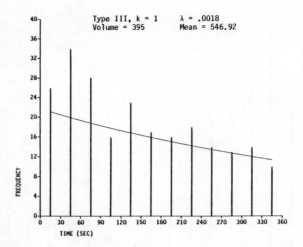

Figure 4-37. Undergraduate Library
Card Catalog — Fall 1981

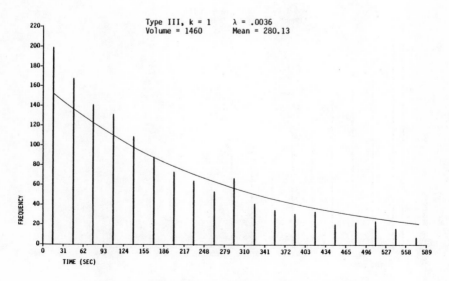

Figure 4-38. Undergraduate Library
Terminals — Fall 1981

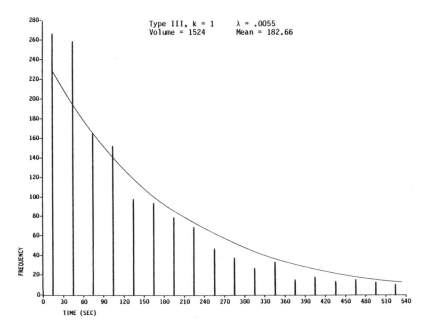

Figure 4-39.   West Campus Library
Card Catalog — Fall 1981

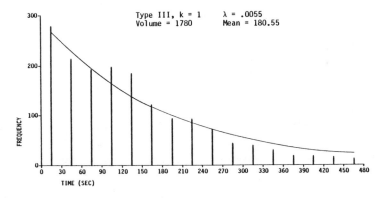

Figure 4-40.   West Campus Library
Terminals — Fall 1981

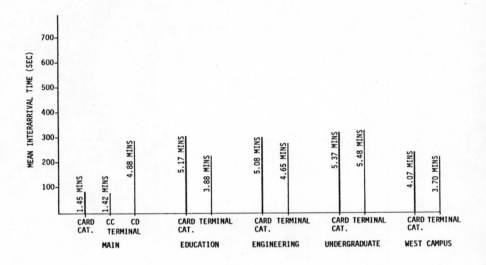

Figure 4-41.   Mean Interarrival Times
Winter 1981

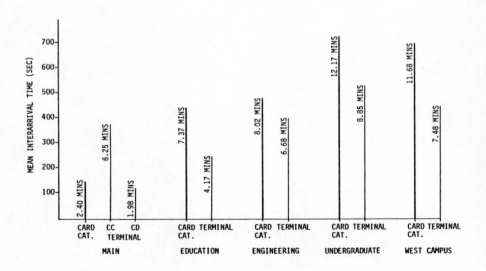

Figure 4-42.   Mean Interarrival Times
Spring 1981

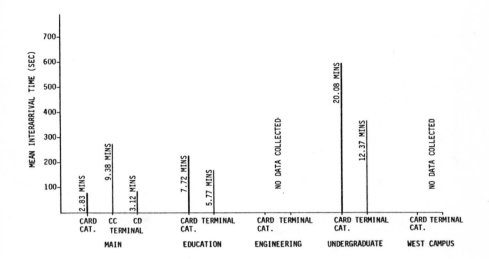

Figure 4-43.   Mean Interarrival Times
Summer 1981

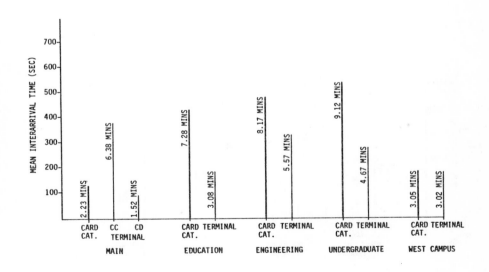

Figure 4-44.   Mean Interarrival Times
Fall 1981

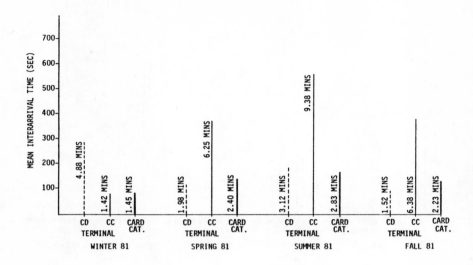

Figure 4-45.   Mean Interarrival Times
Main Library

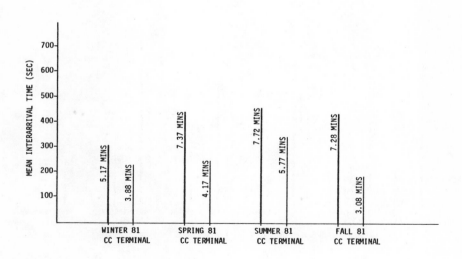

Figure 4-46.   Mean Interarrival Times
Education Library

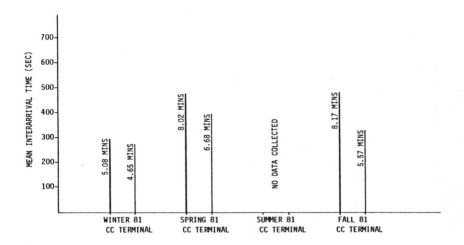

Figure 4-47.   Mean Interarrival Times
Engineering Library

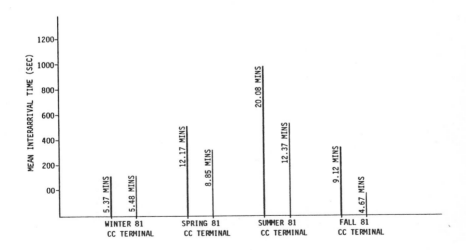

Figure 4-48.   Mean Interarrival Times
Undergraduate Library

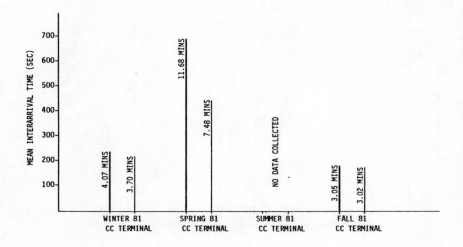

Figure 4-49. Mean Interarrival Times
West Campus Library

TABLES 4-1 TO 4-4

SUMMARY OF TEST RESULTS FOR OBSERVED INTERARRIVALS

Table 4-1. Winter 1981

Library	Type of Distribution	Parameter	Mean of Observed Time, in seconds	Degree of Freedom	Chi-Square	Sample Volume
Main Card catalog	Type III, k = 1	Lamda = .0114	87 (1 min, 27 sec)	13	45	4042
Terminals (card cat.)	Type III, k = 1	Lamda = .0117	85 (1 min, 25 sec)	15	60	3773
Terminals (circ. desk)	Type III, k = 1	Lamda = .0034	293 (4 min, 53 sec)	18	21	969
Education Card catalog	Type III, k = 1	Lamda = .0032	310 (5 min, 10 sec)	19	14	1014
Terminals	Type III, k = 1	Lamda = .0043	233 (3 min, 53 sec)	19	34	1485
Engineering Card catalog	Type III, k = 1	Lamda = .0033	305 (5 min, 5 sec)	18	20	907
Terminals	Type III, k = 1	Lamda = .0036	279 (4 min, 39 sec)	18	36	1076
Undergraduate Card catalog	Type III, k = 1	Lamda = .0031	322 (5 min, 22 sec)	20	94	890
Terminals	Type III, k = 1	Lamda = .0030	329 (5 min, 29 sec)	23	38	1016
West Campus Card catalog	Type III, k = 1	Lamda = .0041	244 (4 min, 4 sec)	15	30	626
Terminals	Type III, k = 1	Lamda = .0045	222 (3 min, 42 sec)	20	20	1131

Table 4-2. Spring 1981

Library	Type of Distribution	Parameter	Mean of Observed Time, in seconds	Degree of Freedom	Chi-Square	Sample Volume
Main						
Card catalog	Type III, k = 1	Lamda = .0070	144 (2 min, 24 sec)	18	88	2816
Terminals (card cat.)	Type III, k = 1	Lamda = .0027	375 (6 min, 15 sec)	23	33	987
Terminals (circ. desk)	Type III, k = 1	Lamda = .0084	119 (3 min, 39 sec)	17	189	3355
Education						
Card catalog	Type III, k = 1	Lamda = .0023	442 (7 min, 22 sec)	21	57	811
Terminals	Type III, k = 1	Lamda = .0040	250 (4 min, 10 sec)	18	97	1535
Engineering						
Card catalog	Type III, k = 1	Lamda = .0021	481 (8 min, 1 sec)	19	55	708
Terminals	Type III, k = 1	Lamda = .0025	401 (6 min, 41 sec)	20	57	932
Undergraduate						
Card catalog	Type III, k = 1	Lamda = .0014	730 (12 min, 10 sec)	15	25	441
Terminals	Type III, k = 1	Lamda = .0019	531 (8 min, 51 sec)	19	45	641
West Campus						
Card catalog	Type III, k = 1	Lamda = .0014	701 (11 min, 41 sec)	9	11	363
Terminals	Type III, k = 1	Lamda = .0022	449 (7 min, 29 sec)	17	29	584

Table 4-3. Summer 1981

Library	Type of Distribution	Parameter	Mean of Observed Time, in seconds	Degree of Freedom	Chi-Square	Sample Volume
Main						
Card catalog	Type III, k = 1	Lamda = .0059	170 (2 min, 50 sec)	15	223	1573
Terminals (card cat.)	Type III, k = 1	Lamda = .0018	563 (9 min, 23 sec)	11	14	453
Terminals (circ. desk)	Type III, k = 1	Lamda = .0053	187 (3 min, 7 sec)	16	67	1432
Education						
Card catalog	Type III, k = 1	Lamda = .0022	463 (7 min, 43 sec)	13	40	501
Terminals	Type III, k = 1	Lamda = .0029	346 (5 min, 46 sec)	16	50	687
Undergraduate						
Card catalog	Type III, k = 1	Lamda = .0008	1205 (20 min, 5 sec)	9	9	121
Terminals	Type III, k = 1	Lamda = .0013	742 (12 min, 22 sec)	6	12	218

Table 4-4. Fall 1981

Library	Type of Distribution	Parameter	Mean of Observed Time, in seconds	Degree of Freedom	Chi-Square	Sample Volume
Main						
Card catalog	Type III, k = 1	Lamda = .0075	134 (2 min, 14 sec)	15	115	2935
Terminals (card cat.)	Type III, k = 1	Lamda = .0026	383 (6 min, 23 sec)	23	44	1048
Terminals (circ. desk)	Type III, k = 1	Lamda = .0110	91 (1 min, 31 sec)	15	205	4570
Education						
Card catalog	Type III, k = 1	Lamda = .0023	437 (7 min, 17 sec)	19	50	828
Terminals	Type III, k = 1	Lamda = .0054	185 (3 min, 5 sec)	16	124	1437
Engineering						
Card catalog	Type III, k = 1	Lamda = .0020	490 (8 min, 10 sec)	15	58	618
Terminals	Type III, k = 1	Lamda = .0030	334 (5 min, 34 sec)	18	52	936
Undergraduate						
Card catalog	Type III, k = 1	Lamda = .0018	547 (9 min, 7 sec)	12	27	395
Terminals	Type III, k = 1	Lamda = .0036	280 (4 min, 40 sec)	21	74	1460
West Campus						
Card catalog	Type III, k = 1	Lamda = .0055	183 (3 min, 3 sec)	18	64	1524
Terminals	Type III, k = 1	Lamda = .0055	181 (3 min, 1 sec)	16	50	1780

Table 4-5. Summary of Interarrival Times and Chi-square Tests

Library	Distribution		Quarters		
		Winter	Spring	Summer	Fall
Main Card catalog	Type III, k = 1				
	Lamda	.0114	.0070	.0059	.0075
	Mean observed time	87 sec (1 min, 27 sec)	144 sec (2 min, 24 sec)	170 sec (2 min, 50 sec)	134 sec (2 min, 14 sec)
	Degree of freedom	13	18	15	15
	Chi-square	45	88	223	115
	Sample volume	4042	2816	1573	2935
Main Terminals (card cat.)	Type III, k = 1				
	Lamda	.0117	.0027	.0018	.0026
	Mean observed time	85 sec (1 min, 25 sec)	375 sec (6 min, 15 sec)	563 sec (9 min, 23 sec)	383 sec (6 min, 23 sec)
	Degree of freedom	15	23	11	23
	Chi-square	60	33	14	44
	Sample volume	3773	987	453	1048
Main Terminals (circ. desk)	Type III, k = 1				
	Lamda	.0034	.0084	.0053	.0110
	Mean observed time	293 sec (4 min, 53 sec)	119 sec (1 min, 59 sec)	187 sec (3 min, 7 sec)	91 sec (1 min, 31 sec)
	Degree of freedom	18	17	16	15
	Chi-square	21	189	67	205
	Sample volume	969	3355	1432	4570

Table 4-5. Summary of Interarrival Times and Chi-square Tests (continued)

Library	Distribution		Quarters			
			Winter	Spring	Summer	Fall
Education Card catalog	Type III, k = 1	Lamda	.0032	.0023	.0022	.0023
		Mean observed time	310 sec (5 min, 10 sec)	442 sec (7 min, 22 sec)	463 sec (7 min, 43 sec)	437 sec (7 min, 17 sec)
		Degree of freedom	19	21	13	19
		Chi-square	14	57	40	50
		Sample volume	1014	811	501	828
Education Terminals	Type III, k = 1	Lamda	.0043	.0040	.0029	.0054
		Mean observed time	233 sec (3 min, 53 sec)	250 sec (4 min, 10 sec)	346 sec (5 min, 46 sec)	185 sec (3 min, 5 sec)
		Degree of freedom	19	18	16	16
		Chi-square	34	97	50	124
		Sample volume	1485	1535	687	1437
Engineering Card catalog	Type III, k = 1	Lamda	.0033	.0021	data not collected	.0020
		Mean observed time	305 sec (5 min, 5 sec)	481 sec (8 min, 1 sec)		490 sec (8 min, 10 sec)
		Degree of freedom	18	19		15
		Chi-square	20	55		58
		Sample volume	907	708		618

Table 4-5. Summary of Interarrival Times and Chi-square Tests (continued)

Library	Distribution		Quarters			
			Winter	Spring	Summer	Fall
Engineering Terminals	Type III, k = 1	Lamda	.0036	.0025	data not collected	.0030
		Mean observed time	279 sec (4 min, 39 sec)	401 sec (6 min, 41 sec)		334 sec (5 min, 34 sec)
		Degree of freedom	18	20		18
		Chi-square	36	57		52
		Sample volume	1076	932		936
Undergraduate Card catalog	Type III, k = 1	Lamda	.0031	.0014	.0008	.0018
		Mean observed time	322 sec (5 min, 22 sec)	730 sec (12 min, 10 sec)	1205 sec (20 min, 5 sec)	547 sec (9 min, 7 sec)
		Degree of freedom	20	15	9	12
		Chi-square	94	25	9	27
		Sample volume	890	441	121	395
Undergraduate Terminals	Type III, k = 1	Lamda	.0030	.0019	.0013	.0036
		Mean observed time	329 sec (5 min, 29 sec)	531 sec (8 min, 51 sec)	742 sec (12 min, 22 sec)	280 sec (4 min, 40 sec)
		Degree of freedom	23	19	6	21
		Chi-square	38	45	12	74
		Sample volume	1016	641	218	1460

Table 4-5. Summary of Interarrival Times and Chi-square Tests (continued)

Library	Distribution		Quarters			
			Winter	Spring	Summer	Fall
West Campus Card catalog	Type III, k = 1	Lamda	.0041	.0014	data not collected	.0055
		Mean observed time	244 sec (4 min, 4 sec)	701 sec (11 min, 41 sec)		183 sec (3 min, 3 sec)
		Degree of freedom	15	9		18
		Chi-square	30	11		64
		Sample volume	626	363		1524
West Campus Terminals	Type III, k = 1	Lamda	.0045	.0022	data not collected	.0055
		Mean observed time	222 sec (3 min, 42 sec)	449 sec (7 min, 29 sec)		181 sec (3 min, 1 sec)
		Degree of freedom	20	17		16
		Chi-square	20	29		50
		Sample volume	1131	584		1780

FIGURES 4-50 TO 4-93
OBSERVED VS. THEORETICAL DISTRIBUTIONS: SERVICE TIMES

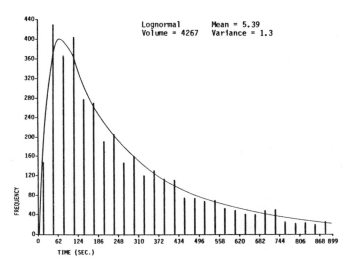

Figure 4-50.   Main Library
Card Catalog – Winter 1981 – Lognormal

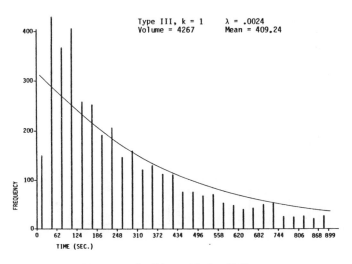

Figure 4-51.   Main Library
Card Catalog – Winter 1981 – Type III

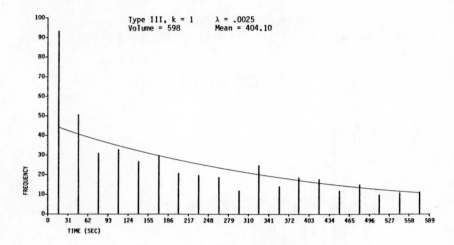

Figure 4-52.   Main Library
Terminals (Card Catalog) — Winter 1981 — Type III

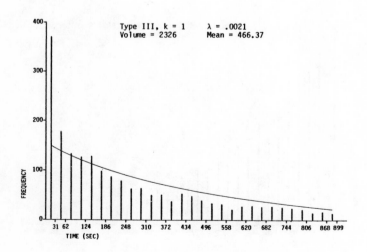

Figure 4-53.   Main Library
Terminals (Circulation Desk) — Winter 1981 — Type III

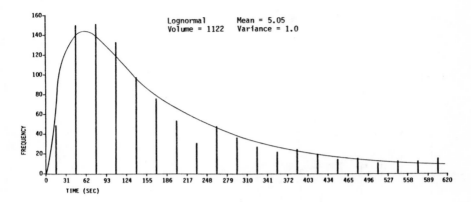

Figure 4-54.   Education Library
Card Catalog — Winter 1981 — Lognormal

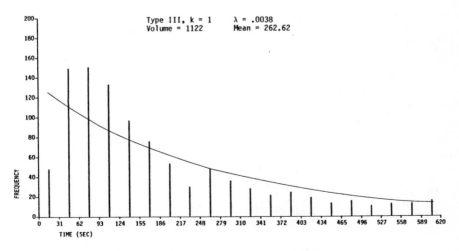

Figure 4-55.   Education Library
Card Catalog — Winter 1981 — Type III

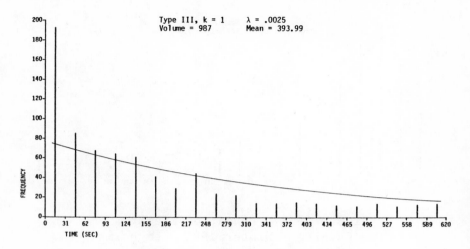

Figure 4-56.   Education Library
Terminals - Winter 1981 - Type III

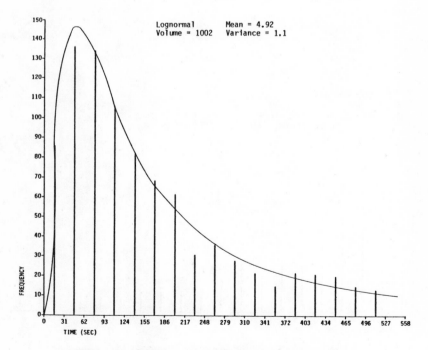

Figure 4-57.   Engineering Library
Card Catalog - Winter 1981 - Lognormal

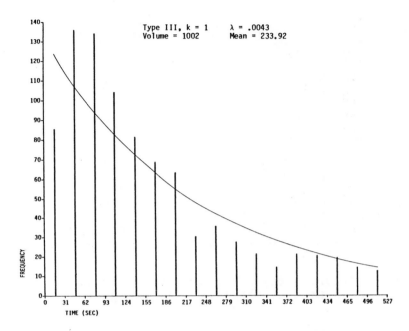

Figure 4-58.   Engineering Library
Card Catalog – Winter 1981 – Type III

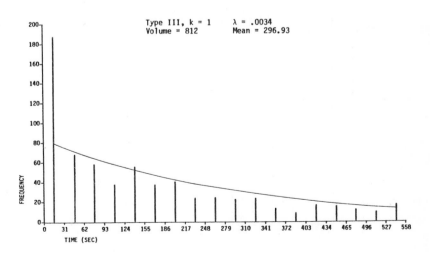

Figure 4-59.   Engineering Library
Terminals – Winter 1981 – Type III

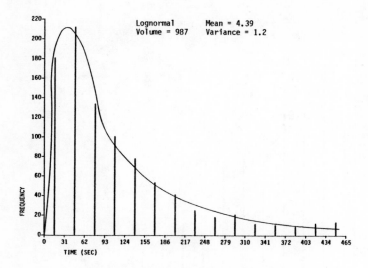

Figure 4-60.   Undergraduate Library
Card Catalog — Winter 1981 — Lognormal

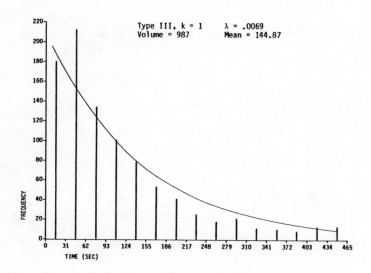

Figure 4-61.   Undergraduate Library
Card Catalog — Winter 1981 — Type III

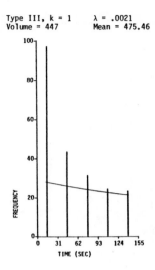

Figure 4-62.   Undergraduate Library
Terminals — Winter 1981 — Type III

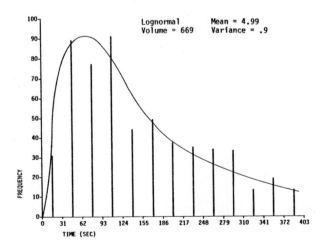

Figure 4-63.   West Campus Library
Card Catalog — Winter 1981 — Lognormal

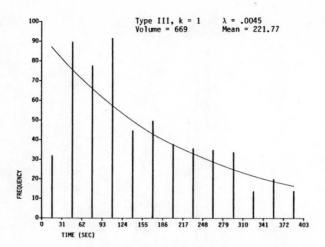

Figure 4-64.   West Campus Library
Card Catalog — Winter 1981 — Type III

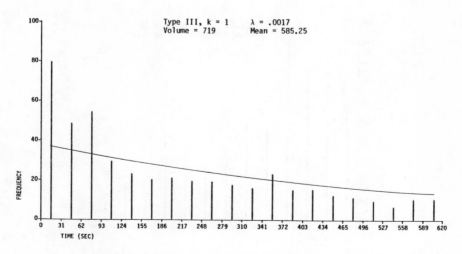

Figure 4-65.   West Campus Library
Terminals — Winter 1981 — Type III

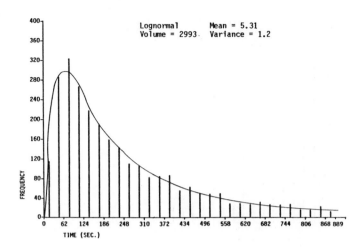

Figure 4-66.   Main Library
Card Catalog – Spring 1981 – Lognormal

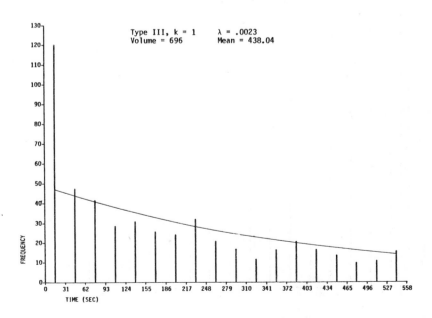

Figure 4-67.   Main Library
Terminals (Card Catalog) – Spring 1981 – Type III

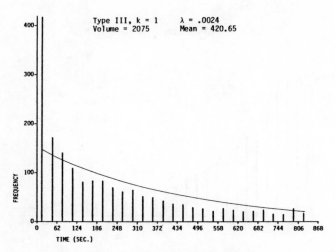

Figure 4-68. Main Library
Terminals (Circulation Desk) – Spring 1981 – Type III

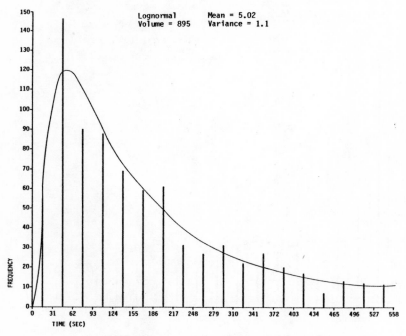

Figure 4-69. Education Library
Card Catalog – Spring 1981 – Lognormal

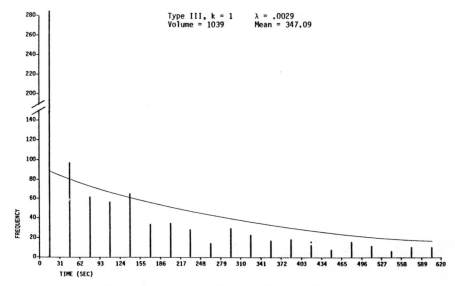

Figure 4-70. Education Library
Terminals – Spring 1981 – Type III

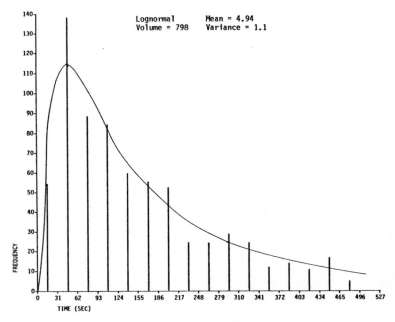

Figure 4-71. Engineering Library
Card Catalog – Spring 1981 – Lognormal

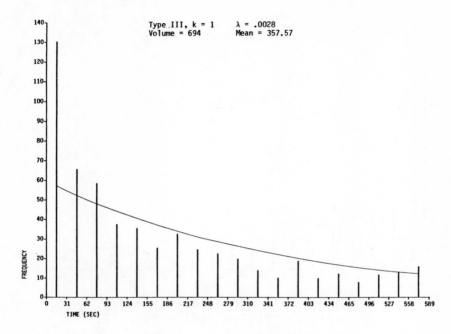

Figure 4-72. Engineering Library
Terminals - Spring 1981 - Type III

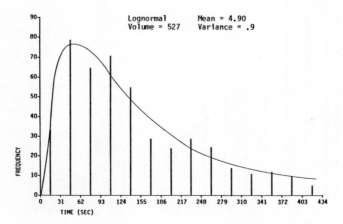

Figure 4-73. Undergraduate Library
Card Catalog - Spring 1981 - Lognormal

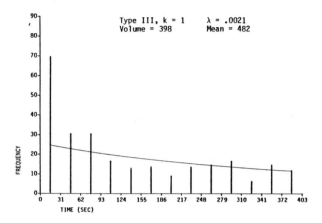

Figure 4-74.   Undergraduate Library
Terminals — Spring 1981 — Type III

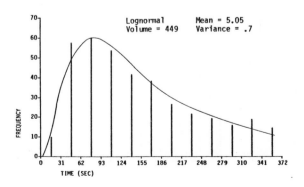

Figure 4-75.   West Campus Library
Card Catalog — Spring 1981 — Lognormal

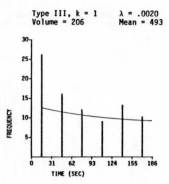

Figure 4-76. West Campus Library
Terminals – Spring 1981 – Type III

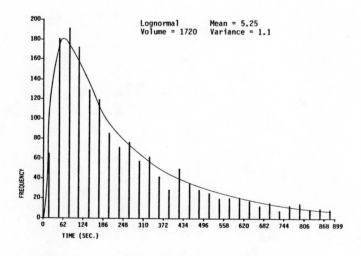

Figure 4-77. Main Library
Card Catalog – Summer 1981 – Lognormal

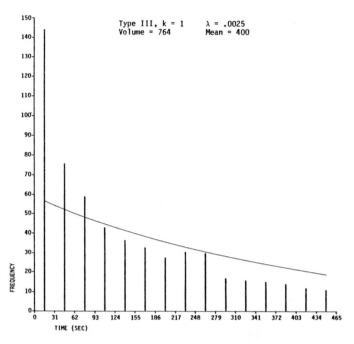

Figure 4-78.   Main Library
Terminals (Circulation Desk) - Summer 1981 - Type III

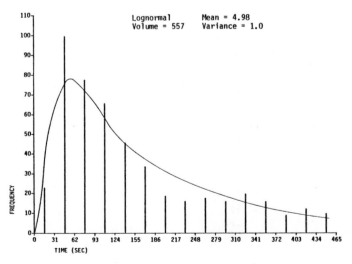

Figure 4-79.   Education Library
Card Catalog - Summer 1981 - Lognormal

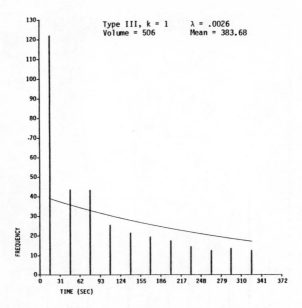

Figure 4-80. Education Library
Terminals — Summer 1981 — Type III

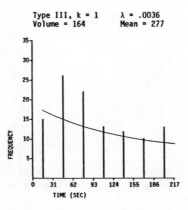

Figure 4-81. Undergraduate Library
Card Catalog — Summer 1981 — Type III

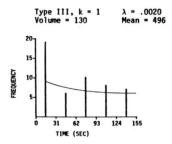

Figure 4-82.   Undergraduate Library
Terminals – Summer 1981 – Type III

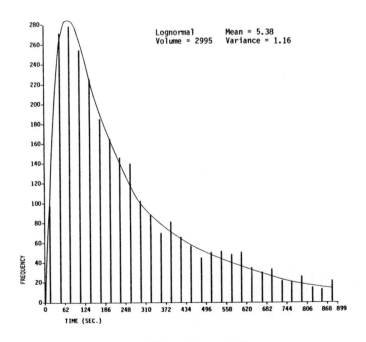

Figure 4-83.   Main Library
Card Catalog – Fall 1981 – Lognormal

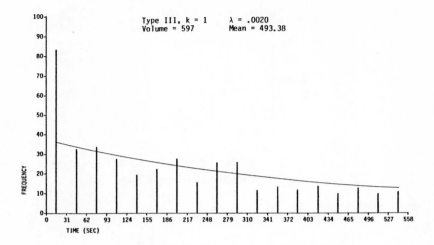

Figure 4-84. Main Library
Terminals (Card Catalog) - Fall 1981 - Type III

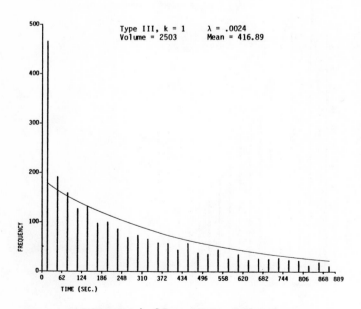

Figure 4-85. Main Library
Terminals (Circulation Desk) - Fall 1981 - Type III

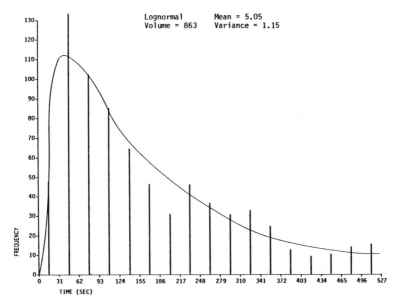

Figure 4-86.   Education Library
Card Catalog - Fall 1981 - Lognormal

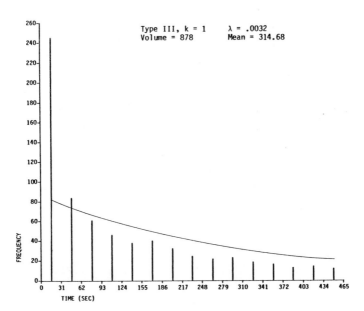

Figure 4-87.   Education Library
Terminals - Fall 1981 - Type III

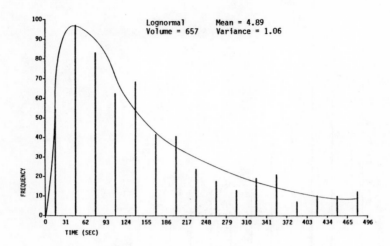

Figure 4-88. Engineering Library
Card Catalog - Fall 1981 - Lognormal

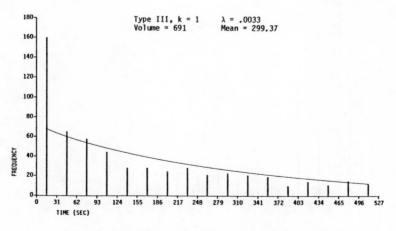

Figure 4-89. Engineering Library
Terminals - Fall 1981 - Type III

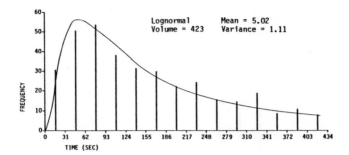

Figure 4-90. Undergraduate Library
Card Catalog – Fall 1981 – Lognormal

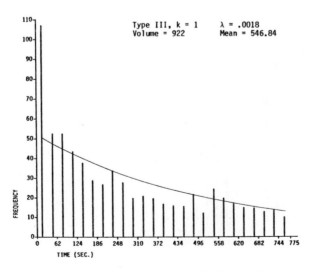

Figure 4-91. Undergraduate Library
Terminals – Fall 1981 – Type III

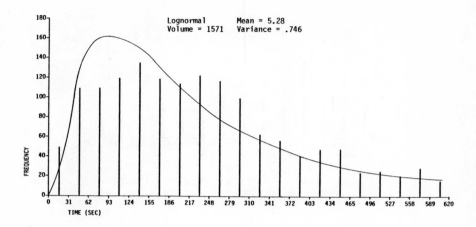

Figure 4-92.   West Campus Library
Card Catalog – Fall 1981 – Lognormal

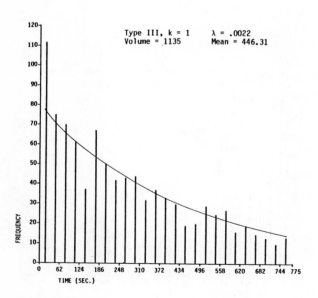

Figure 4-93.   West Campus Library
Terminals – Fall 1981 – Type III

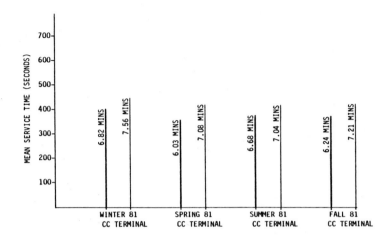

Figure 4-94. Mean Service Times
Main Library

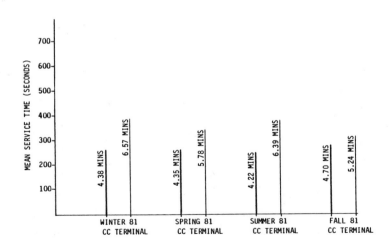

Figure 4-95. Mean Service Times
Education Library

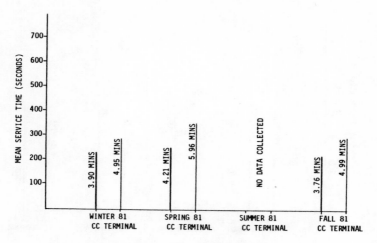

Figure 4-96.   Mean Service Times
Engineering Library

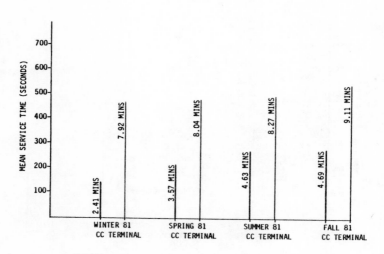

Figure 4-97.   Mean Service Times
Undergraduate Library

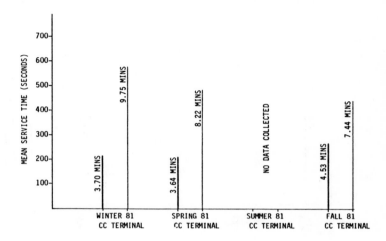

Figure 4-98.   Mean Service Times
West Campus Library

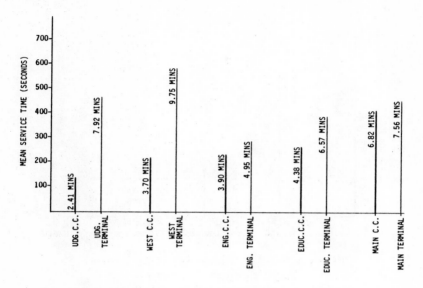

Figure 4-99.   Mean Service Times
Winter 1981

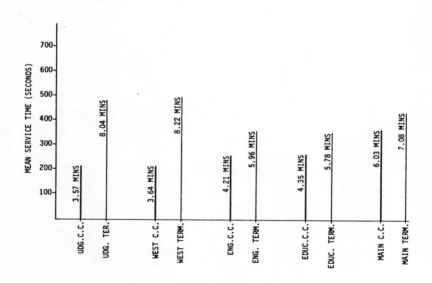

Figure 4-100.   Mean Service Times
Spring 1981

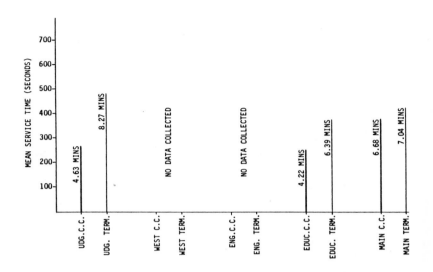

Figure 4-101.   Mean Service Times
Summer 1981

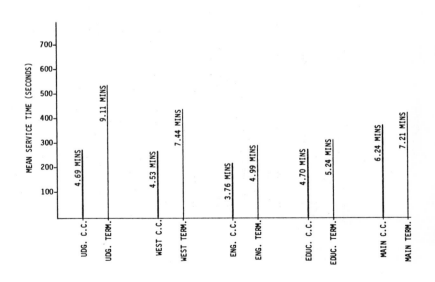

Figure 4-102.   Mean Service Times
Fall 1981

TABLES 4-6 TO 4-9

SUMMARY OF TEST RESULTS FOR SERVICE TIMES

Table 4-6.   Winter 1981

Library	Type of Distribution	Parameter	Mean of Observed Time, in seconds	Degree of Freedom	Chi-Square	Sample Volume
Main						
Card catalog	Lognormal	Mean = 5.39 Variance = 1.3	409 (5 min, 49 sec)	29	66	4267
Terminals (card cat.)	Type III, k = 1	Lamda = .0025	404 (5 min, 44 sec)	19	75	598
Terminals (circ. desk)	Type III, k = 1	Lamda = .0021	466 (7 min, 46 sec)	29	454	2326
Education						
Card catalog	Lognormal	Mean = 5.05 Variance = 1.0	263 (4 min, 23 sec)	21	33	1122
Terminals	Type III, k = 1	Lamda = .0025	394 (6 min, 34 sec)	22	268	987
Engineering						
Card catalog	Lognormal	Mean = 4.92 Variance = 1.1	234 (3 min, 54 sec)	17	15	1002
Terminals	Type III, k =1	Lamda = .0034	297 (4 min, 57 sec)	18	185	812
Undergraduate						
Card catalog	Lognormal	Mean = 4.39 Variance = 1.2	145 (2 min, 25 sec)	15	16	987
Terminals	Type III, k = 1	Lamda = .0021	475 (7 min, 55 sec)	5	217	447
West Campus						
Card catalog	Lognormal	Mean = 4.99 Variance = .9	222 (3 min, 42 sec)	13	20	669
Terminals	Type III, k = 1	Lamda = .0017	585 (9 min, 45 sec)	21	91	719

Table 4-7. Spring 1981

Library	Type of Distribution	Parameter	Mean of Observed Time, in seconds	Degree of Freedom	Chi-Square	Sample Volume
Main						
Card catalog	Lognormal	Mean = 5.31 Variance = 1.2	362 (6 min, 2 sec)	29	34	2993
Terminals (card cat.)	Type III, k = 1	Lamda = .0023	438 (7 min, 18 sec)	18	136	696
Terminals (circ. desk)	Type III, k = 1	Lamda = .0024	421 (7 min, 1 sec)	27	619	2075
Education						
Card catalog	Lognormal	Mean = 5.02 Variance = 1.1	261 (4 min, 21 sec)	18	25	895
Terminals	Type III, k = 1	Lamda = .0029	347 (5 min, 47 sec)	20	546	1039
Engineering						
Card catalog	Lognormal	Mean = 4.94 Variance = 1.1	253 (4 min, 13 sec)	16	24	798
Terminals	Type III, k = 1	Lamda = .0028	358 (5 min, 58 sec)	19	131	694
Undergraduate						
Card catalog	Lognormal	Mean = 4.90 Variance = .9	214 (3 min, 34 sec)	14	12	527
Terminals	Type III, k = 1	Lamda = .0021	482 (8 min, 2 sec)	13	110	398
West Campus						
Card catalog	Lognormal	Mean = 5.05 Variance = .7	219 (3 min, 39 sec)	12	7	449
Terminals		Insufficient data				

Table 4-8. Summer 1981

Library	Type of Distribution	Parameter	Mean of Observed Time, in seconds	Degree of Freedom	Chi-Square	Sample Volume
Main						
Card catalog	Lognormal	Mean = 5.25 Variance = 1.1	341 (5 min, 41 sec)	29	24	1720
Terminals (card cat.)		Insufficient	data			
Terminals (circ. desk)	Type III, k = 1	Lamda = .0025	400 (6 min, 40 sec)	15	182	764
Education						
Card catalog	Lognormal	Mean = 4.98 Variance = 1.0	253 (4 min, 13 sec)	15	28	557
Terminals	Type III, k = 1	Lamda = .0026	384 (6 min, 24 sec)	11	210	506
Undergraduate						
Card catalog		Insufficient	data			
Terminals		Insufficient	data			

Table 4-9. Fall 1981

Library	Type of Distribution	Parameter	Mean of Observed Time, in seconds	Degree of Freedom	Chi-Square	Sample Volume
Main Card catalog	Lognormal	Mean = 5.38 Variance = 1.16	375 (6 min, 15 sec)	29	34	2995
Terminals (card cat.)	Type III, k = 1	Lamda = .0020	493 (8 min, 13 sec)	18	79	597
Terminals (circ. desk)	Type III, k = 1	Lamda = .0024	417 (6 min, 57 sec)	29	588	2503
Education Card catalog	Lognormal	Mean = 5.05 Variance = 1.15	282 (4 min, 42 sec)	17	28	863
Terminals	Type III, k = 1	Lamda = .0032	315 (5 min, 15 sec)	15	385	878
Engineering Card catalog	Lognormal	Mean = 4.89 Variance = 1.06	225 (3 min, 45 sec)	16	17	657
Terminals	Type III, k = 1	Lamda = .0033	299 (4 min, 59 sec)	17	155	691
Undergraduate Card catalog	Lognormal	Mean = 5.02 Variance = 1.11	281 (4 min, 41 sec)	14	9	423
Terminals	Type III, k = 1	Lamda = .0018	547 (9 min, 7 sec)	25	94	922
West Campus Card catalog	Lognormal	Mean = 5.28 Variance = .746	272 (4 min, 32 sec)	23	140	1571
Terminals	Type III, k = 1	Lamda = .0022	446 (7 min, 26 sec)	25	41	1135

Table 4-10. Summary of Service Times and Chi-square Tests

Library	Distribution		Quarters			
			Winter	Spring	Summer	Fall
Main Card Catalog	Lognormal	Mean Variance	5.39 1.3	5.31 1.2	5.25 1.1	5.38 1.16
		Mean observed time	409 sec (6 min, 49 sec)	362 sec (6 min, 2 sec)	341 sec (5 min, 41 sec)	375 sec (6 min, 15 sec)
		Degree of freedom	29	29	29	29
		Chi-square	66	34	24	34
		Sample volume	4267	2993	1720	2995
Main Terminals (card cat.)	Type III, k = 1	Lamda	.0025	.0023	insuf-ficient data	.0020
		Mean observed time	404 sec (6 min, 44 sec)	438 sec (7 min, 18 sec)		493 sec (8 min, 13 sec)
		Degree of freedom	19	18		18
		Chi-square	75	136		79
		Sample volume	598	696		597
Main Terminals (circ. desk)	Type III, k = 1	Lamda	.0021	.0024	.0025	.0024
		Mean observed time	466 sec (7 min, 46 sec)	421 sec (7 min, 1 sec)	400 sec (6 min, 40 sec)	417 sec (6 min, 57 sec)
		Degree of freedom	29	27	15	29
		Chi-square	454	619	182	588
		Sample volume	2326	2075	764	2503

Table 4-10. Summary of Service Times and Chi-square Tests (continued)

Library	Distribution		Quarters			
			Winter	Spring	Summer	Fall
Education Card catalog	Lognormal	Mean	5.05	5.02	4.98	5.05
		Variance	1.0	1.1	1.0	1.15
		Mean observed time	263 sec (4 min, 23 sec)	261 sec (4 min, 21 sec)	253 sec (4 min, 13 sec)	282 sec (4 min, 42 sec)
		Degree of freedom	21	18	15	17
		Chi-square	33	25	28	28
		Sample volume	1122	895	557	863
Education Terminals	Type III, k = 1	Lamda	.0025	.0029	.0026	.0032
		Mean observed time	394 sec (6 min, 34 sec)	347 sec (5 min, 47 sec)	384 sec (6 min, 24 sec)	315 sec (5 min, 15 sec)
		Degree of freedom	22	20	11	15
		Chi-square	268	546	210	385
		Sample volume	987	1039	506	878
Engineering Card catalog	Lognormal	Mean	4.92	4.94	data not collected	4.89
		Variance	1.1	1.1		1.06
		Mean observed time	234 sec (3 min, 54 sec)	253 sec (4 min, 13 sec)		225 sec (3 min, 45 sec)
		Degree of freedom	17	16		16
		Chi-square	15	24		17
		Sample volume	1002	798		657

Table 4-10. Summary of Service Times and Chi-square Tests (continued)

Library	Distribution		Winter	Spring	Summer	Fall
				Quarters		
Engineering Terminals	Type III, k = 1	Lamda	.0034	.0028	data not collected	.0033
		Mean observed time	297 sec (4 min, 57 sec)	358 sec (5 min, 58 sec)		299 sec (4 min, 59 sec)
		Degree of freedom	18	19		17
		Chi-square	185	131		155
		Sample volume	812	694		691
Undergraduate Card catalog	Lognormal	Mean Variance	4.39 1.2	4.90 .9	insufficient data	5.02 1.11
		Mean observed time	145 sec (2 min, 25 sec)	214 sec (3 min, 34 sec)		281 sec (4 min, 41 sec)
		Degree of freedom	15	14		14
		Chi-square	16	12		9
		Sample volume	987	527		423
Undergraduate Terminals	Type III, k = 1	Lamda	.0021	.0021	insufficient data	.0018
		Mean observed time	475 sec (7 min, 55 sec)	482 sec (8 min, 2 sec)		547 sec (9 min, 7 sec)
		Degree of freedom	5	13		25
		Chi-square	217	110		94
		Sample volume	447	398		922

Table 4-10. Summary of Service Times and Chi-square Tests (continued)

Library	Distribution		Quarters			
			Winter	Spring	Summer	Fall
West Campus Card catalog	Lognormal	Mean Variance	4.99 .9	5.05 .7	data not collected	5.28 .74
		Mean observed time	222 sec (3 min, 42 sec)	219 sec (3 min, 39 sec)		272 sec (4 min, 32 sec)
		Degree of freedom	13	12		23
		Chi-square	20	7		140
		Sample volume	669	449		1571
West Campus Terminals	Type III, k = 1	Lamda	.0017	insufficient data	data not collected	.0022
		Mean observed time	585 sec (9 min, 45 sec)			446 sec (7 min, 26 sec)
		Degree of freedom	21			25
		Chi-square	91			41
		Sample volume	719			1135

Table 4-11. Summary of Regression Analysis

	Main	Educ	Engr	Undg	West	Combined	One Slope	Alone
Books out								
R2	.411	.058	.292	.239	.272	.725	.703	.609
Slope	.534	.154	.389	.817	1.161		.467	.629
Intercept	29.470	24.550	10.170	9.700	14.350			11.980
Sample	176.000	177.000	141.000	176.000	134.000	804.000	804.000	804.000
Persons								
R2	.458	.202	.342	.163	.302	.741	.732	.667
Slope	.977	.792	.723	1.320	2.237		.977	1.227
Intercept	29.540	16.380	9.350	10.480	12.900			11.530
Sample	176.000	176.000	141.000	175.000	133.000	801.000	801.000	801.000
Ref desk								
R2	.203	.064*	.052*	.380	.570	.680	.636	.454
Slope	.548	.356	-.117	1.049	.945		.382	.841
Intercept	47.890	27.360	26.950	9.810	21.450			23.130
Sample	141.000	73.000	80.000	31.000	59.000	384.000	384.000	384.000
Circ desk								
R2	NO DATA COLLECTED	.000*	.042*	.279	.346	.330	.270	.079
Slope		.006	.197	.408	.865		.329	.295
Intercept		31.736	19.420	11.210	20.760			20.390
Sample		133.000	80.000	158.000	64.000	435.000	435.000	435.000
Lib Pop								
R2	.525*	.023*	.072*	.019*	.673	THESE ANALYSES NOT CONDUCTED DUE TO LOW SAMPLE SIZE IN 3 OF 5 CASES		
Slope	.107	.061	-.217	.012	.110			
Intercept	25.650	25.380	26.600	19.720	2.242			
Sample	7.000	40.000	3.000	8.000	51.000			
Cards								
R2	.397	.089	.440	.420	.696	.775**	.772	.720
Slope	.664	.478	.802	.813	.811		.705	.971
Intercept	35.350	22.880	8.600	7.929	10.130			10.310
Sample	175.000	173.000	141.000	157.000	131.000	777.000	777.000	777.000

$*p > .01$
**slope heterogeneity not found

Table 4-11. Summary of Regression Analysis
(continued)

	Main	Educ	Engr	Undg	West	Combined	One Slope	Alone
Persons & Cards								
R2	.504	.209	.511	.441	.718			.775
Slope(Persons)	.661	.704	.386	.437	.692			.607
Slope(Cards)	.326	.161*	.598	.747	.731			.595
Intercept	24.800	15.166	5.397	5.775	7.351			7.905
Sample	175.000	173.000	141.000	157.000	131.000			777.000
Books out & Persons								
R2								.667
Slope(Books)								-.003*
Slope(Perspns)								1.234
Intercept								11.502
Sample								804.000
Regression of Persons on Books out								
R2							.933	.915
Slope							.479	.514
Intercept								.342
Sample							884.000	884.000
Regression of Cards on Books out								
R2	.404	.150	.263	.183	.232	.714	.692	.573
Slope	.499	.158	.303	.499	1.102		.424	.535
Intercept	17.390	11.172	7.334	6.316	8.723			5.885
Sample	184.000	179.000	142.000	158.000	135.000	798.000	798.000	798.000
Regression of Cards on Persons								
R2	.459	.212	.290	.117	.236	.729	.715	.641
Slope	.920	.508	.542	.775	2.056		.863	1.049
Intercept	17.013	8.686	7.148	6.956	7.661			5.367
Sample	184.000	180.000	142.000	158.000	135.000	799.000	799.000	799.000

*p > .01
**slope heterogeneity not found

Table 4-12. Probability of Waiting in Queue $\leq$ Time t Is 0.90

Values represent $\lambda/\mu = \rho$ where λ = arrival rate, μ = service rate (or λ · mean service time).

k	tμ 0.2	0.4	0.6	0.8	1.0	1.2	1.4	1.6	1.8	2.0
1	0.12	0.14	0.17	0.19	0.22	0.25	0.28	0.30	0.33	0.36
2	0.59	0.67	0.76	0.85	0.93	1.00	1.06	1.12	1.18	1.23
3	1.21	1.37	1.52	1.65	1.77	1.87	1.96	2.04	2.11	2.17
4	1.91	2.14	2.34	2.52	2.67	2.79	2.90	2.99	3.06	3.13
5	2.66	2.96	3.21	3.42	3.59	3.73	3.85	3.95	4.03	4.11
6	3.44	3.81	4.10	4.34	4.53	4.69	4.81	4.92	5.01	5.08
7	4.25	4.68	5.01	5.28	5.49	5.65	5.79	5.90	5.99	6.07
8	5.08	5.57	5.94	6.22	6.45	6.62	6.76	6.88	6.98	7.05
9	5.92	6.47	6.87	7.18	7.41	7.59	7.75	7.86	7.96	8.05
10	6.78	7.38	7.81	8.14	8.38	8.57	8.73	8.85	8.95	9.04
11	7.65	8.30	8.76	9.10	9.36	9.55	9.72	9.84	9.94	10.03
12	8.53	9.22	9.71	10.07	10.33	10.53	10.69	10.82	10.93	11.02
13	9.42	10.16	10.67	11.05	11.32	11.53	11.69	11.82	11.93	12.01
14	10.30	11.10	11.63	12.02	12.30	12.51	12.68	12.80	12.92	13.01
15	11.21	12.04	12.60	12.99	13.28	13.50	13.66	13.80	13.92	14.00
16	12.11	12.99	13.57	13.97	14.27	14.49	14.66	14.79	14.90	14.99
17	13.02	13.94	14.54	14.94	15.25	15.47	15.64	15.78	15.90	15.99
18	13.94	14.89	15.51	15.93	16.23	16.46	16.64	16.78	16.90	16.98
19	14.86	15.84	16.47	16.92	17.22	17.46	17.64	17.78	17.89	17.98
20	15.78	16.80	17.46	17.90	18.21	18.44	18.62	18.77	18.89	18.98
30	25.13	26.48	27.26	27.78	28.12	28.38	28.58	28.73	28.85	28.95

number of terminals required

Table 4-13. Probability of Waiting in Queue ≤ Time t Is 0.95

Values represent $\lambda/\mu = \rho$ where λ = arrival rate, μ = service rate (or $\lambda \cdot$ mean service time).

k	$t\mu$ 0.2	0.4	0.6	0.8	1.0	1.2	1.4	1.6	1.8	2.0
1	0.06	0.07	0.09	0.10	0.12	0.14	0.16	0.18	0.21	0.23
2	0.41	0.48	0.55	0.63	0.70	0.78	0.85	0.91	0.97	1.03
3	0.93	1.07	1.22	1.35	1.48	1.59	1.69	1.78	1.87	1.94
4	1.54	1.77	1.98	2.16	2.33	2.47	2.60	2.71	2.80	2.89
5	2.22	2.52	2.79	3.02	3.22	3.39	3.53	3.65	3.76	3.85
6	2.94	3.32	3.64	3.92	4.14	4.33	4.48	4.62	4.73	4.82
7	3.70	4.14	4.52	4.82	5.07	5.28	5.44	5.58	5.70	5.80
8	4.47	4.99	5.41	5.75	6.02	6.24	6.41	6.55	6.68	6.78
9	5.27	5.86	6.32	6.68	6.97	7.20	7.38	7.54	7.66	7.77
10	6.08	6.74	7.24	7.63	7.93	8.16	8.36	8.52	8.64	8.75
11	6.91	7.62	8.17	8.58	8.89	9.14	9.33	9.50	9.63	9.74
12	7.75	8.52	9.10	9.54	9.86	10.11	10.32	10.49	10.62	10.74
13	8.61	9.44	10.05	10.50	10.84	11.10	11.30	11.47	11.61	11.72
14	9.46	10.36	11.00	11.47	11.81	12.07	12.29	12.46	12.61	12.71
15	10.33	11.27	11.95	12.43	12.78	13.06	13.27	13.45	13.59	13.70
16	11.21	12.21	12.90	13.39	13.77	14.05	14.26	14.43	14.58	14.71
17	12.09	13.14	13.85	14.37	14.75	15.03	15.25	15.43	15.57	15.70
18	12.98	14.06	14.81	15.34	15.72	16.01	16.25	16.42	16.57	16.69
19	13.86	15.01	15.78	16.32	16.71	17.00	17.24	17.42	17.56	17.69
20	14.77	15.96	16.74	17.30	17.70	17.98	18.22	18.41	18.55	18.68
30	23.91	25.51	26.50	27.14	27.57	27.91	28.15	28.36	28.51	28.64

number of terminals required

Table 4-14. Probability of Waiting in Queue $\leq$ Time t Is 0.99

Values represent $\lambda/\mu = \rho$ where λ = arrival rate, μ = service rate (or $\lambda \cdot$ mean service time).

k	tμ 0.2	0.4	0.6	0.8	1.0	1.2	1.4	1.6	1.8	2.0
1	0.01	0.01	0.02	0.02	0.03	0.03	0.04	0.05	0.05	0.06
2	0.18	0.21	0.25	0.30	0.35	0.40	0.46	0.52	0.58	0.64
3	0.52	0.61	0.71	0.83	0.94	1.05	1.16	1.27	1.36	1.45
4	0.97	1.14	1.32	1.50	1.67	1.83	1.98	2.11	2.24	2.35
5	1.50	1.75	2.00	2.25	2.47	2.67	2.85	3.01	3.15	3.28
6	2.09	2.42	2.75	3.05	3.32	3.55	3.76	3.94	4.09	4.23
7	2.72	3.14	3.53	3.89	4.20	4.46	4.69	4.88	5.04	5.19
8	3.39	3.89	4.35	4.75	5.10	5.38	5.63	5.83	6.01	6.16
9	4.08	4.67	5.19	5.64	6.01	6.32	6.57	6.79	6.97	7.13
10	4.80	5.47	6.05	6.54	6.94	7.26	7.53	7.76	7.95	8.11
11	5.54	6.29	6.93	7.45	7.88	8.21	8.50	8.73	8.93	9.09
12	6.29	7.12	7.82	8.37	8.82	9.18	9.47	9.70	9.91	10.07
13	7.06	7.97	8.72	9.30	9.77	10.14	10.44	10.68	10.89	11.06
14	7.84	8.84	9.62	10.24	10.72	11.11	11.41	11.66	11.87	12.05
15	8.64	9.70	10.53	11.18	11.68	12.08	12.39	12.65	12.86	13.03
16	9.44	10.58	11.46	12.13	12.65	13.05	13.37	13.62	13.84	14.03
17	10.27	11.46	12.38	13.08	13.61	14.02	14.35	14.62	14.84	15.01
18	11.09	12.36	13.32	14.04	14.59	15.01	15.33	15.60	15.82	16.00
19	11.92	13.25	14.26	15.00	15.55	15.98	16.31	16.59	16.82	17.00
20	12.76	14.16	15.21	15.96	16.53	16.96	17.31	17.58	17.81	17.98
30	21.43	23.44	24.75	25.68	26.33	26.82	27.18	27.50	27.74	27.93

number of terminals required

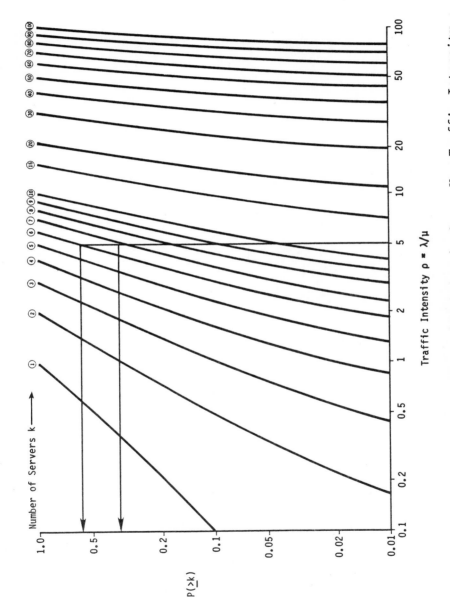

Figure 4-103. Probability of Waiting in Queue Vs. Traffic Intensity ρ

Guidelines for Conducting a Terminal Requirements Study

5.1 Introduction and Scope

These guidelines are given to assist library managers in conducting a computer terminal requirements study for their own libraries or library systems. This chapter summarizes the necessary steps to conduct a terminal requirements study. It is not the intent to explore the mathematical background, the methodologies, the assumptions made, or the background of the assumptions in detail here, but to outline the methodologies tested in the research as examined and discussed in the previous chapters.

These guidelines are intended primarily for use where there is insufficient staff available to conduct a full-scale research effort. However, the steps necessary to conduct the full-scale research are outlined; thus, the guidelines are equally applicable where sufficient personnel are available to conduct such an effort. In the second case especially, it is recommended that the expertise of someone who is familiar with the techniques of systems analysis be available either within or outside the organization conducting the study. Such assistance can save time, effort and money.

A summary of the required steps in conducting a terminal requirements study is shown in Figure 5-1. What follows is a general outline of the minimum tasks

to be accomplished, with a summary of the procedures
to be followed. These guidelines are presented with
the expectation that time can be saved by gathering
the required data and analyzing it in this
successfully pretested format. Data collection and
analysis, and the methodology form the basis of these
guidelines and will provide an orderly approach to the
solution of the terminal requirements problem.

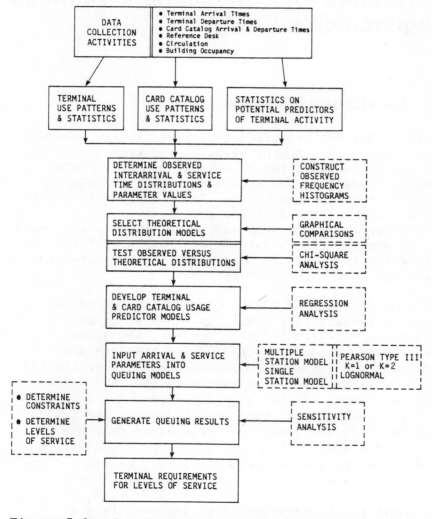

Figure 5-1.   Required Steps in Conducting a Terminal
                Requirements Study

5.2 Organizational Requirements

Planning organizational requirements for a terminal
requirements study is essential for the successful
completion of data collection and analysis. Personnel
must be selected and provided with the proper amount
of training, particularly for data collection.
Layouts of libraries must be determined to plan data
collection locations. Time periods to be measured
must be determined, based on staff experience and
knowledge of the library's usage patterns; peak
activity periods should be sampled. The most
important point is determining what questions need to
be answered and ensuring that the people involved are
made aware of these, whether through formal training,
memo, briefing, or other means.

The structure for computer files must be divided and
programmed, goals established, and the desired end
products determined. The process from data collection
through analysis should be well documented for
possible future use.

5.3 Methodology and Analysis Procedures

This task consists of collecting the appropriate data
to measure the use of the library, as well as the
editing, processing, and statistical analysis of the
observed data.

5.3.1 Data Collection

Assessment of library use can be based on four aspects
of patron activity:

1. Reference and directional questions asked at the
    reference and circulation desks;
2. Building occupancy;
3. Time spent by patrons searching at the card
    catalog (service times); and, if applicable,
4. Service time at the terminals.

Data collection at the reference and circulation
desks, along with building occupancy counts, may be
done by regular staff. Since recording service time
at the card catalog and at the terminals requires
constant monitoring for a given period, it is probably
not feasible to use regular on-duty staff. Thus
temporary help or regular staff not on desk duty may
be needed to perform this task.

Data should be collected for representative periods of
the day on activity at reference and circulation
desks, and at entrance and exit gates to determine
building occupancy. Service times at the card catalog
and/or terminals should be collected at peak activity
times. Two-hour blocks of time appear to be the
amount needed to get an adequate reading on service
patterns, and the maximum time data collectors can
work accurately.

Data collection forms and equipment such as stop
watches, clip boards, etc., must be provided. The
collection forms should be developed or adapted from
the samples illustrated in Chapter 2. These forms
must be designed with data recording, entry, and
analysis in mind. It should be easy to record the
needed information from the observers' point of view,
and the forms should facilitate subsequent data entry
and analysis. All three needs of recording, entry,
and analysis can be satisfied by keeping the forms
simple and uncluttered and by careful planning.

Thorough briefing of data collectors (staff and/or
temporary personnel) prior to starting actual data
collection will eliminate the need to include any but
the briefest instructions on the form, if any are
needed at all. Pretesting forms allows the bugs to be
worked out before data collection begins, thus
precluding the need for forms to be altered during the
course of the study. This, in turn, allows for easier
and more reliable observation, data entry, and
analysis.

To aid data collectors in recording their
observations, the forms should leave as little as
possible to the discretion of the individual observer,
and should be organized in a familiar format whenever
possible. If an observer simply checks or leaves
blank a particular column of incidental information,
there is less distraction from the main task. For
example, at the card catalog the main task is to
record accurate start and stop times for a given
patron's search.

The data collection tasks at the reference and
circulation desks may be similarly simplified if the
staff have collected data on reference and directional
questions for the Higher Education General Information
Survey (HEGIS), since the form used to collect HEGIS
data may be used almost without alteration for a
queuing study. Activity at the reference and
circulation desk areas should be measured in the same
way as is done for HEGIS: reference and directional
questions are recorded after the patron leaves. Data
collection periods may be as short as 15 minutes, but
hourly blocks are preferable for most data needs.

Building occupancy can be determined for any given
hour by comparing the cumulative total of exits and
entrances. The difference between the two indicates
the total number of patrons in the library during the
hour in question.

Given that increasing numbers of libraries have
security systems, most libraries have an existing
means of counting the arrivals and departures of
patrons. For libraries that do not, or for those
whose counters are not reliable, other devices need to
be installed. Electronic beams are accurate, and can
be mounted anywhere, but are expensive. Digital
counters attached to turnstiles or pressure mats
attached to counters may be used. Whatever device is
used, it should be thoroughly pretested before the
study begins.

Collecting readings from the entrance and exit gate
counters need only be done on a regular basis; in the

queuing study data was collected hourly. Opening and
closing counts should also be recorded to determine
how many patrons are in the library during the first
and last hours of business.

Service time at the card catalog should be based on
clearly defined start and stop times. If the catalog
has restricted access (i.e., one or two doors leading
into a room housing only the catalog), numbers can be
given to patrons as they enter and the time recorded.
Patrons can then return the numbers, and the end time
be recorded as they leave.

In cases where the catalog may be approached from any
number of directions, observations must be more
direct. In this setting, start time is recorded when
a patron first opens the card drawer. End time is
recorded when the patron physically leaves the area.
This eliminates for the observer the problem of trying
to determine whether the patrons are starting a
different search if they go to another drawer, or
whether they are continuing the same search.

In a busy catalog area, descriptive information is
needed so that the observer can keep track of several
patrons at once. If the catalog is large enough to
have several aisles, an observer is assigned to each
aisle with the responsibility only for start and end
times of patrons within the observer's section. In
this case, a fairly detailed description of the patron
is required, so that if the patron continues the
search in another aisle, and thus is timed by more
than one data collector, the total search time can
later be determined by matching the description and
ending time with the subsequent starting times from
the various observers.

If personnel and time permit, a reliability check may
be included in the catalog studies for larger
libraries. For reliability, an observer selects one
patron at a time and follows the patron through an
entire search, regardless of how many aisles are
entered. This provides a reading of how much lag time
occurs when a person goes from aisle to aisle and also

provides some indication of accuracy of the service
times recorded by the other observers.

Service time for activity at the terminals should be
based on clearly defined start and stop times. A
search could be considered to start when the patron
touches the keyboard, and to end when the patron
leaves the terminal. Since there may be more than one
person at the terminals, descriptive information will
be useful. Also, if terminal service time is to be
matched with computer transaction tapes, terminal ID's
should be recorded to match the ID number assigned by
the system, to aid in later analysis.

5.3.2 Data Analysis, Model Selection, and Application

The first task to be completed after the data
collection phase is the observed data analysis, which
inputs directly into the selection of the theoretical
probability distribution functions. Data should be
collected on the arrival and service patterns at both
the card catalog and the terminals. Data reduction
requires calculation of the interarrival times, i.e.,
the time periods between successive arrivals at the
service location (catalog or terminal), and the
service times, i.e., the length of time service is
provided to the patrons (catalog or terminal).

Upon completion of these calculations, observed
frequency histograms should be constructed as
discussed in Chapter 4. The shape of these observed
patterns are then studied to determine if the Pearson
Type III model (k = 1 or k = 2) or the Lognormal model
is appropriate. Such frequency histograms should be
constructed and examined both for arrival patterns
(interarrivals versus frequencies) and service
patterns (service times versus frequencies).

Testing of the observed patterns with the theoretical
models should then proceed using a chi-square analysis
comparing observed frequencies with expected
(theoretical) frequencies. The results of the
chi-square analysis will provide a measure of the
models' fit.

At this stage, model selection is determined either by
observed data analysis or by the assuming that the
models presented are representative. If data is not
gathered to verify demand and service patterns, the
recommendation is to assume the negative exponential
(Pearson Type III, k = 1) model for arrival and
service patterns, as this will allow use of the
queuing models as presented in Chapter 3.

The terminal demand (that is, arrival rate at the
terminal) is then required along with service rate,
for input to the queuing analysis. If this study is
replicated at a location with terminals, the data
collection activity will produce both the mean
interarrival times and the service times for use as
input.

Where terminals are not available or the library is
designing for future demand levels, regression
equations may be utilized to predict terminal demand.
These equations take the form shown in Chapter 3. It
is suggested that regression equations be developed
for the appropriate library systems, if feasible, with
the staff and skills available. Such equations should
consider the potential predictors of terminal use:
circulation activity, reference activity, and building
occupancy.

In this study, the best results were obtained using
only circulation activity as a predictor, and this is
recommended. However, if other predictors work for
the library under consideration then they should be
used. Corresponding regression equations for the
individual libraries may also be developed if
feasible. In our case, the R^2 values were lower than
those obtained in aggregating the libraries and then
obtaining the regression. For this reason, it is
recommended that the data be aggregated over all
library types, and also be compared with the equations
obtained from individual libraries regressed over the
independent variables, if new regression equations are
developed at the individual library level.

The output of the chosen regression equation will
serve as input to the queuing models, i.e., the
arrival rate λ. The required service rate may be
obtained from the mean service times from Tables 4-6
through 4-9 in Chapter 4. If terminals are already
present, mean service times may be determined from
direct observation.

Once the arrival and service distributions have been
determined along with values for the required
parameters, the remaining task consists of inputting
this information into the queuing models and
determining the required number of terminals for the
chosen levels of service (as shown by the examples in
Chapter 4).

Equations for the queuing analysis for both the single
service station and the multiple service stations
situations are shown in Table 3-2 and Table 3-3 in
Chapter 3. These assume negative exponential (random)
arrival and service patterns. They may be programmed
for running on a computer rather than by hand.

Alternatively, Tables 4-11 through 4-13 and Figure
4-103 may be used to obtain the required number of
terminals for the determined conditions and level of
service chosen, i.e., acceptable time delays and the
probability of such delays occurring. Examples using
these tables and figures are found in Chapter 4.

5.4 Conclusions

These guidelines have been presented to serve as a
condensed procedures manual to be used when carrying
out a terminal requirements study. They should be
utilized along with the detailed methodologies
discussed in the other chapters of this monograph. In
some cases, it may not be necessary to refer to the
other chapters, depending upon the experience of the
individuals conducting the study, the data that is
available, and the level of effort that is available.
In any case, these guidelines provide managers with an
outline of the required procedures.

A reliable estimate of the number of terminals required is important since nearly every library is faced with limited funding. The methodology should be used and supplemented with the knowledge available from individuals closely associated with the particular library system under study. The end results of applying these techniques will be both the avoidance of long lines of patrons waiting to use the online catalog and the elimination of over purchase of terminals which may be idle and which cost money.

The extensive data collection effort and testing of the models reported in this monograph provide a sound foundation supporting the theoretical representation of terminal activity. Thus one can proceed with a degree of confidence in the predictive power of the models presented. Although the models may be assumed a priori, only actual observed data can verify their representativeness. Observed data from five libraries at one institution has been presented so that those interested may consider it along with their own systems.

This monograph coordinates and consolidates all the required material into one package. The statistics, theory, and mathematics are all here for those who wish to explore them. The use of these techniques should greatly assist in making decisions when planning for terminal requirements in libraries.

Data Collection Handbook

DATA COLLECTION PROCEDURES

Card Catalog

1. You are responsible for getting the starting and ending times for all patrons who enter the catalog (or your section of it) during the time of your shift. Don't worry about keeping track of patrons who were there before you started, or who are still there after you finish.

2. Before you begin, fill out the upper portion of the form completely. Make sure you fill in the correct date. "STARTING TIME" refers to the time you start your shift, not when you start a new form.

    For those working the card catalog in the Main Library, make sure you indicate the aisle in which you are observing: Aisle 1 is closest to the exit; Aisle 2 is in the middle; Aisle 3 is closest to the Circulation Desk.

3. A search begins when the patron pulls out a drawer for the first time and continues until he or she leaves the immediate catalog area. The patron may look at more than one drawer during the course of

her/his search, so DO NOT give that person a new
entry each time he/she goes to another drawer. Do
not depend on that person's returning a drawer to
its proper place to signal an end to the search:
patrons often don't put things back; if a patron
leaves the immediate catalog area, log him or her
out.

4. For those working at the Education, Engineering,
West Campus, and Undergraduate Libraries: the
description section on the form is simply so you
can keep track of who is at the card catalog, as
there is frequently more than one patron using the
catalog at a time. Write down whatever
information you need to accomplish that purpose.

For those working the Main Library card catalog:
since in most cases you will be unable to watch
the entire catalog, you must put down as much
description as possible, so that patrons may be
traced to another section if they don't complete
their search in yours. To aid in this tracing,
indicate where the patron goes after he/she leaves
your section in the space provided on the form.
Also, assign a number to each patron that comes
into your section; if that patron returns, just
put the number where the description would be to
save time.

5. Digital watches will be provided to record the
time. They will be attached to the clipboard
on which you will be writing. DO NOT REMOVE THEM.
Record the complete time as displayed: hours,
minutes, seconds (do not use "military time"). Do
not reset the watches, even if they are not
synchronized with the wall clocks or your own
watch. They are set by the LCS internal clock and
are monitored daily.

LCS Terminals

1. You are responsible for getting the starting time
of patrons using the terminals, and this must be

as accurate as possible. Each terminal has a
number attached to it which you will be able to
see clearly. Record the number of the terminal
and the starting time for each patron.

2. Before you begin, fill out the upper part of the
    form completely. Make sure you fill in the
    correct date. "STARTING TIME" refers to the time
    you start your shift.

    For those working the Main Library: because there
    are 25 terminals to be observed in the main
    terminal area, and these are usually quite busy,
    two people will be assigned to observe. There are
    also three or four terminals (depending on time of
    day) to be covered out in the card catalog. One
    person will be assigned to observe these under
    normal circumstances during the week. On
    weekends, those watching the card catalog will
    also keep track of these terminals (the area is
    less busy on weekends).

3. A terminal search begins when the patron puts
    her/his hands on the keys and not before. A
    search ends when the patron leaves the terminal
    for any reason. The patron may go for help, or
    may go to check the Library of Congress Subject
    Heading Guide. If he/she should return, give the
    patron a new entry.

    A finish time is not needed for the terminal
    obervations. The data you record will be matched
    with tapes of terminal activity kept by the
    library. Putting the two pieces of information
    together will allow us to determine how many
    transactions per person occurred during the
    observation period. In essence, the tapes provide
    a finishing time for each patron.

4. Since you are recording only a small amount of
    information for each patron, you will be expected
    to be extremely accurate in recording starting
    times. This is critical, especially during a busy
    observation period.

5.   Digital watches will be provided to record the time. <u>They will be attached to the clipboard on which you will be writing</u>. <u>DO NOT REMOVE THEM</u>. <u>Record the complete time as displayed</u>: hours, minutes, seconds (do not use "military time"). Do not reset the watches, even if they are not synchronized with the wall clock or your own watch. They are set to the LCS internal clock and are monitored daily.

6.   If LCS should go down during your observation period, don't leave. It may come back up after a short time. If it does, indicate someplace on the coding sheet the approximate time it went down and the time the system came back up.

For All Data Collectors

1.   Library staff members do use both the card catalog and the LCS terminals from time to time; however, we are only interested in keeping track of non-library staff users. Learn who are library staff members in your respective libraries, and do not include them in the data collection. Student workers in the catalog can be easily identified: they carry small boxes of cards to be used in updating the cards in the catalog. The other library staff members you will learn to identify as you collect data during your shift. If you are in doubt as to whether or not a person is library staff go ahead and record the information, indicating in the margin that the person might be a staff member.

2.   Occasionally there will be two people working together at the catalog or the terminal. For simplicity's sake, keep track of the person who is in physical contact with the cards or the terminal only. If one of the two people is a staff member make sure you record the fact that the patron has received help.

3. Indicate only once if the patron has received
    help. We do not need to know when or how often
    help was sought or given, we only need to know
    that it was received.

4. Under no circumstances are you to talk with
    fellow coders. If a person stops to ask you what
    you are doing, tell them you can't talk now and
    refer them to a library staff member. If a friend
    stops by to chat, tell him/her you can't talk now
    and will see him/her later. If things get slow,
    do not read, your full attention should be on
    collecting data. It is easy to miss a body if you
    are talking or reading.

5. If you can't make it for whatever reason, call
    Susan Miller and the head librarian or supervisor.
    Please give us as much warning as possible so we
    can have your station covered. This is especially
    important for those working weekend and evening
    shifts.

6. If someone does not show, inform the head
    librarian or supervisor. If it is not too busy,
    cover both catalog and terminals yourself. If it
    is too busy, cover one or the other and request a
    student worker from the head librarian to help you
    out.

    For those covering the Main Library: make sure
    the main terminal area is covered. If you are one
    coder short, card catalog coders will also cover
    the terminals in their aisle. If you are two
    coders short, the individual who normally does the
    reliability check should take up a permanent aisle
    location.

7. You may decide among yourselves who covers what.
    However, you may be moved if Pat Hartsel or Susan
    Miller think you would be more effective
    elsewhere.

8. Make sure clipboards and watches are all secured
    before you leave. Several watches have already
    been stolen.

9. Make sure time sheets are filled out and signed.
    You won't get your paycheck on schedule if you
    forget to sign the time sheet. Time sheets will
    be located at your respective libraries.
    Paychecks may be picked up at the Personnel Office
    in the Main Library.

Maps

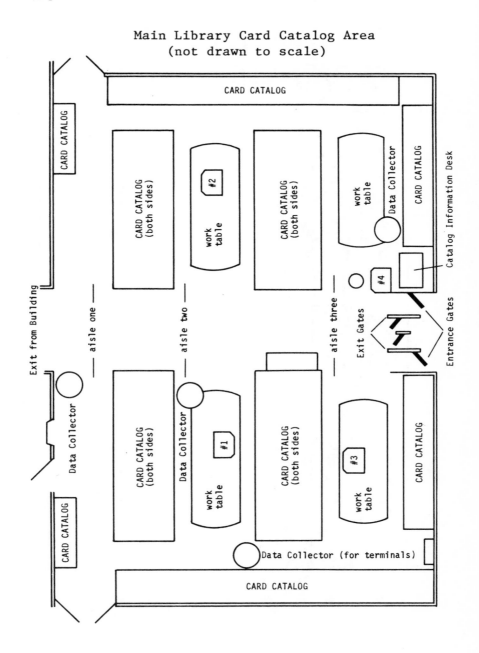

Main Library Card Catalog Area
(not drawn to scale)

Main Library Terminal Area
(not drawn to scale)

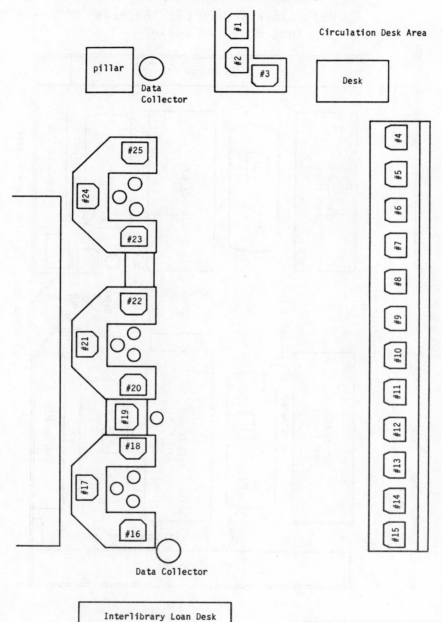

Education Library
(not drawn to scale)

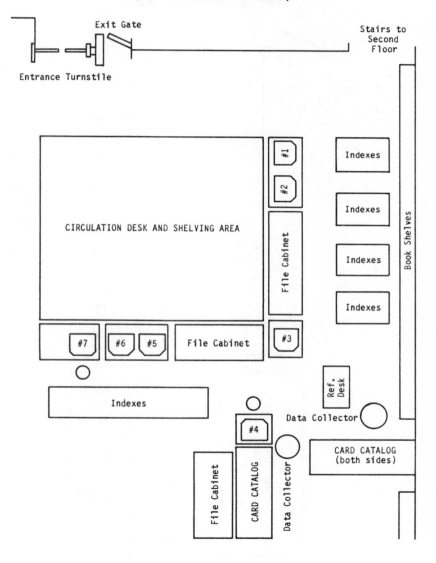

Engineering Library
(not drawn to scale)

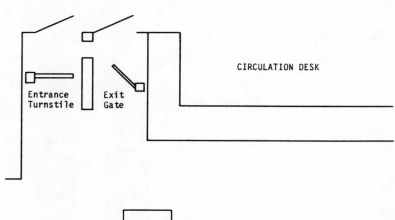

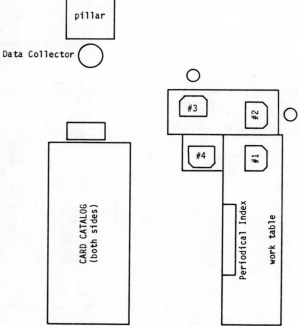

Undergraduate Library
(not drawn to scale)

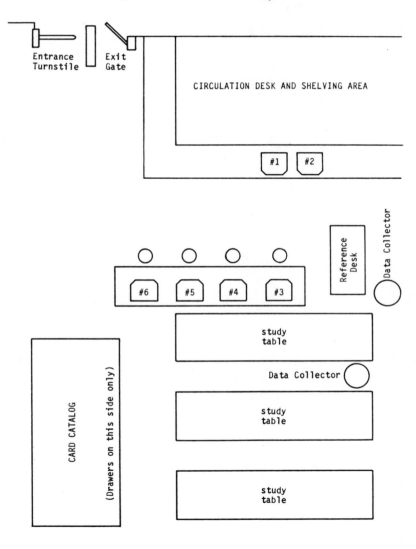

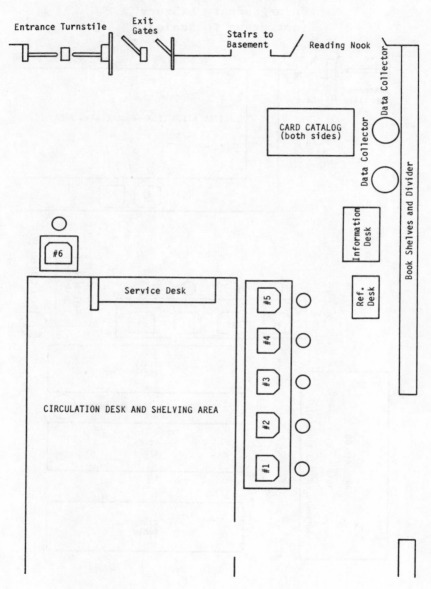

West Campus Library
(not drawn to scale)

Selected References

Aitchison, J.; Brown, J.A.C. The lognormal distribution, with special reference to its uses in economics. Cambridge, Eng.: Cambridge University Press; 1969.

Analysis of some queuing models in real-time systems. IBM data processing techniques GF20-0007-1. White Plains, NY: IBM Corporation; 1971.

Au, Tung; Shane, Richard M.; Hoel, Lester A. Fundamentals of systems engineering; probabilistic models. Reading, MA: Addison-Wesley Publishing Co.; 1972.

Cox, D.R.; Smith, Walter L. Queues. London: Methuen and Co. Ltd.; 1961.

Feller, William. An introduction to probability theory and its applications. Volume I. New York: John Wiley and Sons; 1950.

Hogg, Robert V.; Craig, Allen T. Introduction to mathematical statistics. 2d ed. New York: Macmillan Co.; 1965.

Kreyszig, Erwin. Introductory mathematical statistics: principles and methods. New York: John Wiley and Sons; 1970.

Meyer, Paul L. Introductory probability and statistical applications. Reading, MA: Addison-Wesley Publishing Co.; 1965.

Tolle, J.E. Vehicular headway distributions: testing and results. Transportation Research Record. 567: 56-64; 1976.

Weslowsky, George O. Multiple regression and analysis of variance: an introduction for computer users in management and economics. New York: John Wiley and Sons; 1976.

Whitney, D. Ransom. Elements of mathematical statistics. New York: Holt, Rinehart and Winston; 1961.

Index

Arrival
  observed distribution, 24
  patterns, 57
  rate, 24
  theoretical, 25, 26
  volume, 24
  SEE ALSO Interarrival time

Building occupancy (gate count)
  data collection
    counting devices in, 13, 139
    forms, 14
    methodology, 13, 139-140
  reliability as predictor of
    terminal use, 3
  terminal usage regressed on,
    55-56

Card catalog, data collection
  forms, 17
  methodology
    defining start and end times,
    15, 140
    reliability check, 18, 140
    user description information
    in, 16, 140
Chi-square analysis, goodness of
  fit, 23, 33, 141
Circulation activity
  data collection
    forms, 11, 12
    methodology, 11, 138, 139
  reliability as predictor of
    terminal use, 3, 142
  terminal usage regressed on,
    54-56
Coefficient of variation, 49
Correlation coefficient, 36-37

Data collection
  forms, 12, 14, 17, 19
    development of, 10, 138-139
    use of, 11, 15-16, 18, 138-139
    user description information
    in, 15-16, 140
  equipment, 138
  methodology
    building occupancy, 13, 138,
    139-140
    card catalog, 15-18, 140
    reference and circulation
    desks, 11, 138, 139
    terminals, 18-21, 141
    training for, 10-11, 137
Data reduction, 141
Demand, system, and system
  capacity, 4-6, 38

Erlang distribution, 27

Gamma function, 26, 27
Gate count. SEE Building occupancy
Geometric distribution
  mean, 42
  variance, 42

HEGIS (Higher Education General
  Information Survey), 139
Histogram, observed data frequency
  24, 25, 51, 52, 141

Interarrival time
  average, 24
  defined, 24
  mean, 52
  observed distribution, 24

Level of service
  considered in system analysis, 6
  designing for, 39
Lognormal distribution, 28-31
  mean of, 29
  parameter estimation, 33
  variance of, 29

Maximum likelihood estimators. SEE
      Parameter estimation
Method of least squares, 36, 54
Models
  application, 23-24
  confirmation of reliability, 4,
      23, 51
  queuing, 40-42, 48-50, 57, 143
  testing, 33-34, 52, 53, 141
Moment generating function, 32

Negative exponential, 28, 40
  distribution, 27-28, 32, 43
  mean of, 32
  parameter estimation, 32
Normal distribution, 27, 30
  mean of, 29
  parameter estimation, 29
  variance of, 29

Online catalog. SEE Terminals

Parameter estimation
  maximum likelihood estimators,
      32
  mean, 33
  variance, 33
Patterns
  arrival, 57
  service, 57
Peak activity times, determining,
      10, 137
Pearson Type I distribution,
      inapplicability of, 26
Pearson Type III distribution
  mean, 28
  parameter estimation, 27, 32-33
  variance, 28
Poisson arrivals, 32, 40
Probability distribution,
      selection of, 25-26, 141-142
  SEE ALSO Arrival, observed
      distribution; Service,
      observed distribution

Queuing
  discipline, 40, 57
  models, 40-42, 48-50, 57, 143
  multiple server, 45-48
  single server, 40, 45
  system, 39
    analysis for, 39-40
    theory, 38
Queues
  development of, causes, 4, 6,
      38-39
  dissipation of, 4

Random arrivals. SEE Poisson
      arrivals
Reference activity
  data collection
    forms, 11-12
    methodology, 11, 138, 139
  reliability as predictor of
      terminal use, 3
  terminal usage regressed on,
      55-56
Regression analysis, 34, 53-54
  applicability, 54
  coefficients, 36-37
  data aggregation in, 37-38, 142
  equations, 34-38, 142-143
  R^2 value, 37, 55-56

Scatter diagram, 36, 54
Sensitivity analysis, 34
Service
  observed distribution, 25
  rate, 25
  time
    average, 25
    data collection periods, 9, 10
    defined, 25
    mean, 53
    observed distribution, 25
  patterns, 57
  volume, 25
System
  analysis
    level of service in, 6
    tasks in, 4, 7
  capacity, and system demand,
      4-6, 38
  improving, to avoid queues, 6
  oversaturated, 6
  undersaturated, 6

Terminal requirements study
  staff needed, 135, 137
  steps in conducting, 136–143
Terminal
  data collection
    forms, 19
    defining start and end
      times for, 18, 20–21, 141
    user description information
      in, 18
  hopping, 20–21
  usage regressed on building
    occupancy, 55–56
  usage regressed on number of
    persons checking out books,
    54–56
  usage regressed on reference
    desk activity, 55–56
Traffic intensity, 42–43

User description information
  in card catalog data
    collection, 16, 140
  in terminal data collection, 18

Variables, predictor, choosing,
  35
Volume
  arrival, 24
  service, 25

Waiting time
  distribution, 43–44
  probability, 59

226877